CREATING PLACES

THE WORK OF ARCHER & BUCHANAN ARCHITECTURE

JAMES B. GARRISON

Foreword by JEFF GROFF

Edited by HENRIKA DYCK TAYLOR

MOMENTS / 136

MATERIALS & DETAILS / 178

ARCHIVE / 212

Selected Work from 1996–2021

COLLEAGUES / 224

Alumni to Present

ACKNOWLEDGMENTS / 226

CREDITS / 228

FOREWORD

FOR OVER FIFTY YEARS I have studied the houses of Philadelphia's Main Line suburbs and Chester County, especially the notable country places that defined the area both architecturally and as a way of life. To fully understand this regional architecture I look to the works of architects such as R. Brognard Okie, Wilson Eyre, Charles Barton Keen, and Mellor & Meigs. During the Fifties, Sixties and Seventies, large estates along the Main Line were broken up, vast tracts of land became developed for suburban housing, and little was built of distinction other than the carefully planned houses and landscapes of the architect, Walter Durham. The occasional large house by a noted mid-century architect like Vincent Kling or Richard Neutra proved a rare exception. My lectures regularly referenced the Main Line and its iconic houses—carefully designed and crafted—as a thing of the past. Many of these splendid residences I admired from bygone times became known as white elephants. Some become schools or clubs or lifecare community manor houses. Others came down. I gave talks about the past and a golden age of architectural design never to be seen again.

But in the 1990s I started witnessing something surprising. New houses were going up. Not the so-called McMansions, but homes that were fairly large, well-designed, and detailed. Thoughtfully placed in the landscape, these new houses echoed the best of the country place era not simply as copies of the past, but as residences crafted for modern families. There were some liberties taken with design vocabulary, but proportion, scale, and sensitive use of material and color characterized the structures. Consistently, I saw signs on many of the best houses under construction that read "Archer & Buchanan Architecture Ltd."

As I got to know Peter Archer and Richard Buchanan, I realized they not only had a passion for traditional architecture and the history of the area, but a true understanding of the underlying design principles that make a good building. They immersed themselves in studying earlier examples, traveling as the great Philadelphia architects of the past did to see and sketch and photograph. Peter and Richard took inspiration from notable English architects such as Voysey and Lutyens and applied vocabulary and the way dramatic lines and contrasting materials were used to great effect to the regional work of their firm. Somehow, they found the craftsmen who could create the details that are at the heart of a successful building. The long-held cliché that "they don't build them like that anymore" vanishes when you see Archer & Buchanan's Arts & Crafts residence in Berwyn or Bryn Coed Farm in Chester Springs.

Restoration, additions, and alterations always pose a challenge. How much original fabric should be kept? How to upgrade systems and provide modern comforts while maintaining the essential qualities of the original building? Is an addition distinctive or does it blend in? Often a setting is quite changed—diminished land, surrounding development, or a desire for a different landscape style may be contributing factors. A conversation between all the elements is needed and the successful architect is the conductor bringing together house, interior design, landscape setting, garden, and outbuildings. In the latter in particular, creativity and whimsy reign as seen in the Hobbit House or in the transformation of an 1898 stable in Wayne, which preserved the character and delight of that earlier structure while making a completely modern residence.

On my bookshelf today are a variety of architectural monographs from the 1920s including the work of Wallace & Warner, Mellor, Meigs & Howe, and Harrie Lindeberg. I go back to them often to understand the design of that era, to simply enjoy the variety and visual appeal, and also to imagine a different time and place and life in those houses. This book will take a well-deserved place on that shelf and evoke a similar feeling as it reveals a second golden age of country house architecture in the Philadelphia area and beyond.

— *Jeff Groff, Estate Historian at Winterthur Museum, Garden & Library*

June 2021

INTRODUCTION

THE ART OF MAKING PLACES through architectural design and building is timeless. Although twenty-five years has passed in the blink of an eye, Archer & Buchanan Architecture has produced an extraordinary body of work that is a testament to a truly collaborative process involving clients, architects, and other design and building professionals. The firm's portfolio avoids trends yet responds to changes in the way we live to create places of enduring value. What then, might differentiate this work from others in the same market-place? The answers are subtle and will become evident as the reader takes in the imagery from selected projects and reads the accompanying essays which address the consistent themes in the oeuvre of the firm.

Starting an architectural practice is a daunting undertaking: part leap of faith, part a conviction that there is demand for a particular approach to design with clientele who will make it sustainable. A thriving practice depends on an understandable offering to clients and the ability to deliver. From the outset, Archer & Buchanan focused on the fundamentals of architectural design to achieve residential projects that delighted their clients. Success led to growth and the practice eventually began to include institutional, planning, and historic preservation commissions. The founding principles evident in the earliest works have expanded to accommodate changes in lifestyle and technology but remain true to the firm's original philosophy. Staying fresh means being open to projects of different sizes and building types for the opportunities they represent in terms of client dialogue, variety in construction, and development of deep collaboration in the office between the younger and more senior members of the firm.

True custom residential design is highly nuanced and requires combining all the skills and discipline of other building types. Client relationships become personal via levels of discourse uncommon to other architectural typologies and depend on open and professional communication. Having a practice with a regional focus also helps in having some common ground with prospective clients and builders. A shared cultural sensibility can be a conversation starter towards understanding the landscape, the context, and expectations.

Southeastern Pennsylvania and Philadelphia have a particularly rich heritage in architecture and design. The region's design culture emanates from William Penn's initial settlements, which assimilated into a new colony founded on the principles of religious tolerance; promotion of commerce, science, and education; and a prescient sense that the quality and stewardship of the land would lead to continuing prosperity. Residential design was an intrinsic component and by 1900, Philadelphia had established itself as a leader in design and publications related to the American Home. The tumultuous events of the mid-twentieth century, however, put a damper on further developments in architect-designed custom homes, but by the 1980s a new generation of architects began to see real opportunity in residential architecture. Many of the works published in this thirty-year, post-World War II era, especially in *Architectural Record*'s annual "Record Houses," were vacation residences, but more year-round houses with considerable stylistic variety also began to appear.

From this rich milieu of regional tradition, demographic change, and possibility, Peter Archer and Richard Buchanan founded their firm in 1996. They realized there was a local clientele for custom residential architecture, and not the kind of fully optioned production homes which then dominated the market. New York architect, Robert A. M. Stern, contributed to a new moment for the design of houses with his iconic revival of the 100-year-old shingle style for homes in the Hamptons a few years before. In his preface to the 1991 book, *The American Houses of Robert A. M. Stern*, he writes "The American single-family house is a dream house...the American household, given even modest means, creates a "home" that is much more than shelter..."

These aspirations endure but need the right circumstances to really propagate. The founding partners of Archer & Buchanan envisioned how a collaborative and design-centered practice could take root and prosper. Indeed, it grew to include non-residential project types based on the same ideas, but which brought different problems to solve. From the beginning, the work drew its stylistic inspiration from many sources but never to the extent that it could be categorized as "New Traditional" or any other blanket category. For a young practice, there was a deep well of creativity based on an innate feeling for local design context and its precedents. The rural vernacular and suburban development of the early twentieth century became touchstones for Archer & Buchanan's new buildings while additions and alterations emerged from extant cues deftly mixed with inventive forms.

It is always tempting to look at a firm's catalog and begin attributing projects to a particular partner or designer based on architectural style. The work of Archer & Buchanan Architecture, however, is indicative of a honed collaborative approach. Specializations do exist that address the technical aspects of certain project types. Forte in institutional or equestrian design might be led by principals or senior staff, but project teams circulate throughout the full range of work, adding a bottom-up as well as top-down approach to the design and documentation of projects.

There are strong common links in the resumes and backgrounds of the principal leadership with interests in sustainability, history, and community service. These interests are closely intertwined and form a practice ethic independent of style or building type. There is a priority for the firm's works to engage and enhance communities. This lofty goal is actually achieved by a sense of modesty in the design process, even for the largest of projects. The buildings designed by Archer & Buchanan belong as much to the greater context of their settings as they do to their clients. To work in this manner is to guide clients to a result that not merely fits in but complements its locale.

What makes Archer & Buchanan Architecture special is more about method than a signature style. To paraphrase the firm's own statements, "Our strength is in the rich portfolio of projects achieved over the years through meaningful design and client-focused service... Our work reflects a strong appreciation of each client's unique traditions...whether in urban, suburban, or rural settings." The key word in this text is "appreciation." It speaks to a degree of humility as well as the process of inquiry. There is a clear link between these assertions, the approach, and the results.

A couple of project examples bring these links into focus. The new offices for E. B. Mahoney Builders in Bryn Mawr tested a new zoning ordinance drafted to preserve the village character of one of the few older commercial areas on the Main Line. The building program was carefully developed to fit into the massing envelope and its primary street façade pays homage to other commercial buildings with its large windows and entrance details. It further exemplifies the client's reputation for fine craftsmanship by employing handsome brick masonry and ornamental metalwork. This collaborative effort between the architect, client, and local officials culminated in a structure that contributes to its larger context.

A recent residence near Chadds Ford exhibits a design approach that is fresh but informed by examples from the past.

The brick façade with ornamental patterns references nearby precedents in the Bryn Mawr historic district.

Preservation projects contain many interesting details that also can be inspirations for features in new work.

Traditional homes and barns are foils for contemporary additions and interventions.

In the residential arena, preserving and enriching local heritage does not constrain the firm's creativity or a client's wishes when the commission involves existing buildings by a significant architect. In two different projects, which include buildings by noted turn-of-the-century Philadelphia architect, William Price, Archer & Buchanan responded to each with solutions that met client needs while also preserving essential features of the buildings and ensuring continued use for generations to come. One was a carriage house in which the large interior of the former stables and carriage storage became living space with the exterior doors and windows gently modified for residential use. The other building is a larger house that required preservation of its interiors and exterior. Interior alterations were limited to the kitchen and service area to accommodate modern appliances and lifestyle while being indiscernible from the exterior.

Finally, the firm has undertaken many projects in open spaces under conservation easements, which sometimes limit what can be done with new or existing buildings. In several projects around Unionville, existing farm structures and houses have been restored or rebuilt to return the landscape to its traditional use yet are updated to support current requirements or processes. New buildings on open land have been sited for minimal impact while providing expansive views for the owners.

The four essays that accompany the project pages within this volume look at the themes evidenced in the body of work. These themes overlap with each other and might be more strongly expressed in some projects over others, but taken as a whole, they help explain how a diverse group of projects are united. The first essay, "Nature," describes how the work responds to its settings and how sustainability is about more than the conservation of natural resources. It is also about using architecture to preserve and build on the stories of a place. "Context" is about meaning. It describes how established landscapes, buildings, and materials inform the design process in subtle and more overt ways. "Moments" explores the essential spark that ignites a project, bringing it to life. The design process at Archer & Buchanan provides those instances that capture and distill the larger content. "Materials and Details" is the last essay. Here is where the parts and pieces are put together. Raw and highly finished materials combine through details to form the actual building. These essays, like the design process itself, illuminate projects from different aspects to provide a lens for appreciating the work.

Twenty-five years of practice is just one chapter in Archer & Buchanan's story. The world is different now than in 1996, but design as a means for improving quality of life and the built and natural environment has not changed. Architectural design remains a process of observation, inquiry, and dialogue that results in a three-dimensional realization. The collaborative workplace that Archer & Buchanan has established will endure. There is more to come. The work demonstrates a vision wide enough to accept change but focused enough to realize that some fundamental concepts never do.

Photography by: Tom Crane Photography, James B. Garrison, Archer & Buchanan Architecture

ARTS & CRAFTS RESIDENCE

Berwyn, Pennsylvania

THIS ARTS & CRAFTS INSPIRED residence is designed to minimize site disturbance and cultivate a sense of timelessness within the landscape. The first of several commissions over a period of twelve years, the hilltop site was originally occupied by a nineteenth-century country house with magnificent views overlooking acres of undisturbed meadow and backed by dense woods. The program called for a new home that would embody care and craft at every level for a family of six, with additional cottage accommodations suitable for grandparents. Drawing upon Arts & Crafts precedents, the residence showcases the region's most talented artisans and craftsmen who contributed the millwork, art glass, plaster, masonry, and ironwork. The result is a unified melding of art and architecture.

The later addition of the "Cor-Ten Cattails" was originally conceived as a yard sculpture to accompany the house but the design evolved to became a fence to deter deer. Comprised of 300 eight-foot above-grade Cor-Ten self-weathering steel blades set nine inches apart, the fence weaves throughout the front yard, opening and closing around trees in a deliberate serpentine layout. The angular profile of the stanchions and the winding plan can project a wave effect of light passing through or play tricks on the eye; from some points the fence looks solid, from others scalpel thin.

The standalone garage was designed for the display and storage of fine automobiles. The timber frame and masonry beautifully complements the Arts & Crafts style pebble-dash residence. Built into an earthen bank, the garage also provides conventional storage accessible from a lower level. The clear span timber frame—with roof lantern and glass-filled openings on four sides—creates an expansive, light-filled space for the owner's collection.

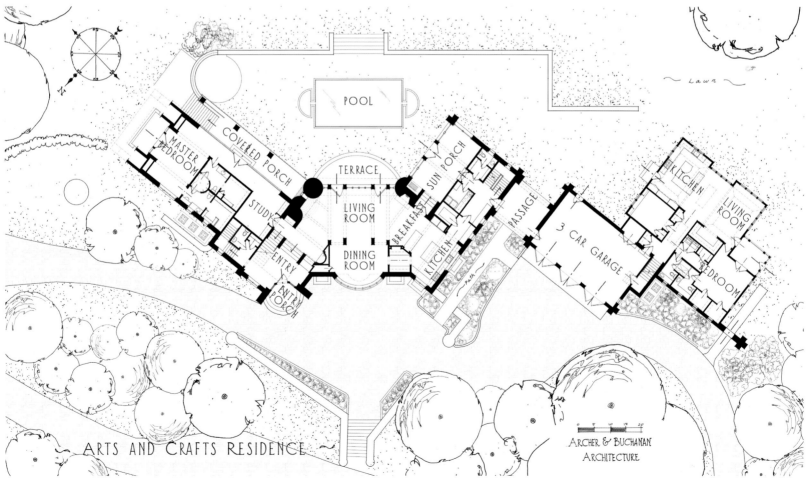

ARTS AND CRAFTS RESIDENCE

ARCHER & BUCHANAN
ARCHITECTURE

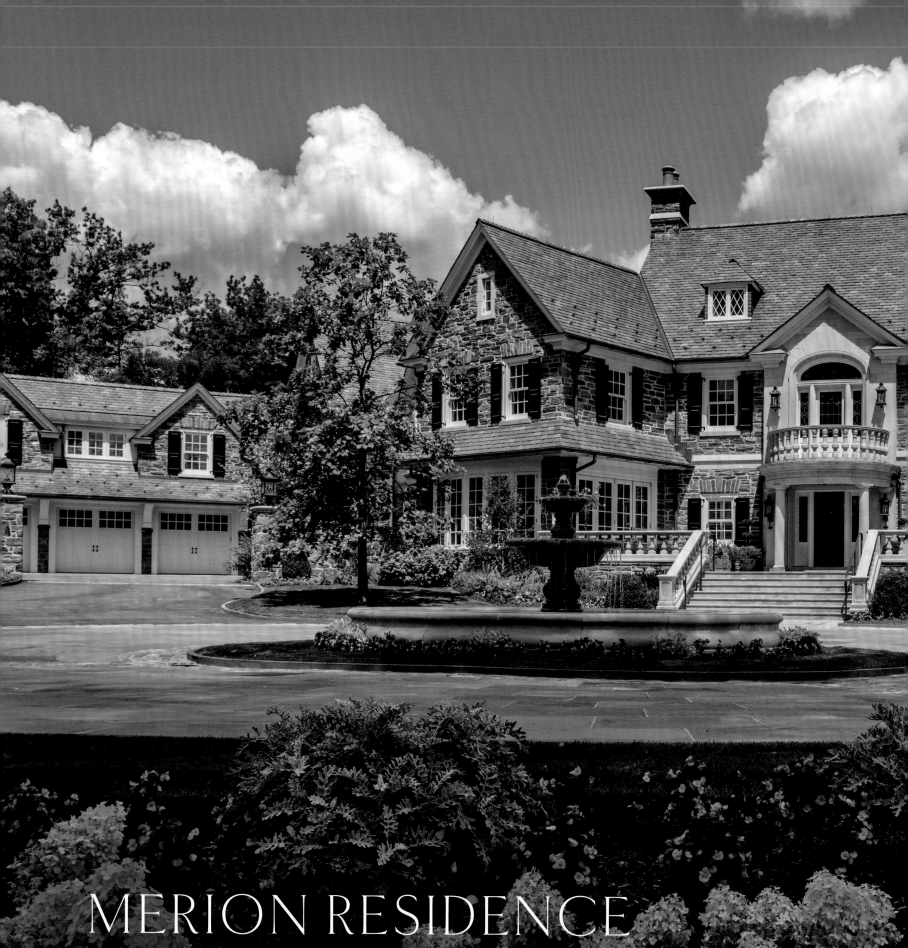

MERION RESIDENCE

Merion Station, Pennsylvania

A TRADITIONAL BUTTERFLY PLAN for this large home in Merion makes the most of a corner site. The design aligns the main entrance with a diagonal line to the street intersection which focuses attention on the forecourt and entry while diminishing the overall size as seen from the street. A division of spaces on the first floor differentiate formal entertaining from family living. There are clear routes between the major rooms with supporting functions nested in the irregular shapes created by the "knuckles" in the overall layout. The formal spaces display exceptional design and craftsmanship in the woodwork, ornamental plaster, light fixtures, and floor finishes.

The exterior impression is consistent with the other early-twentieth-century residences in the neighborhood in terms of size and use of materials such as mica schist and ornamental limestone. While the formal façades facing the streets present classic forms, the garden elevations are inventive and feature an unexpected center bracketed gable over a two-story bay where the arched second floor windows wrap the corners. The design for this residence brings together elegant, historically referenced exteriors and interiors with a plan creatively adapted to twenty-first century living.

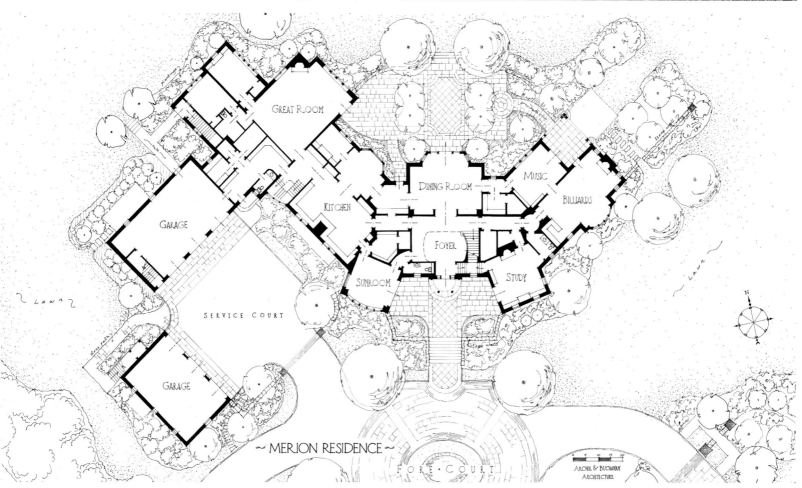

~ MERION RESIDENCE ~

KOHELET YESHIVA LAB SCHOOL

Merion Station, Pennsylvania

THE KOHELET YESHIVA LAB SCHOOL (KYLS) provides a K-8 curriculum to complement the existing 9-12 High School. A private Jewish day school, KYLS integrates an experience-based learning pedagogy with deep immersion in Judaic studies. Hands-on learning experiences, group and collaborative project assignments, and intense use of technology reinforce the school's focus. The educational environment comprises large, open, multi-grade classrooms supported by small group instruction spaces and learning commons. The Middle School curriculum revolves around three primary spaces: the STEAM (Science, Technology, Engineering, Art, Math) Lab, the humanities center, and the Beit Midrash, the space dedicated to religious education and prayer.

The 34,800-square-foot facility includes a cafeteria, administrative offices, dedicated teacher work areas embedded in the learning spaces, and spacious corridors and stairs for social interaction and the display of the children's work.

The siting, scale, and character of the design was influenced by the site context, the client's program, township zoning and the concerns of residential neighbors. The resulting building establishes a presence on a prominent corner without overwhelming the houses that remain in the neighborhood. Use of stone and a variety of window groupings relate the structure to adjacent public and institutional buildings as well as a former mansion, which is the central building of the campus.

Principal in Charge: Dan Russoniello, AIA, LEED AP

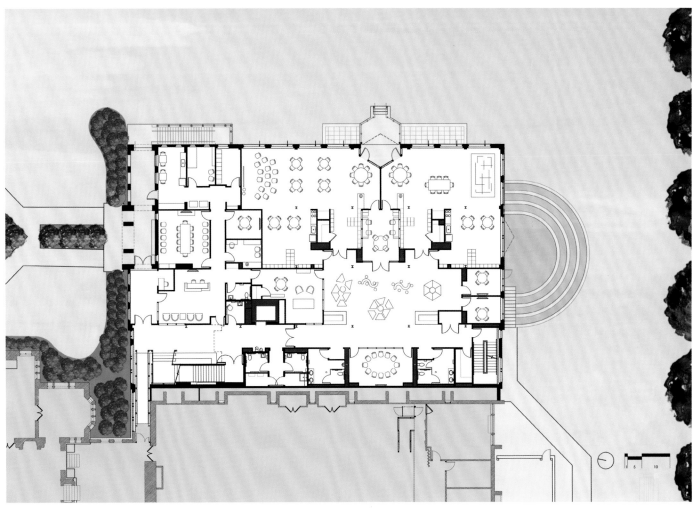

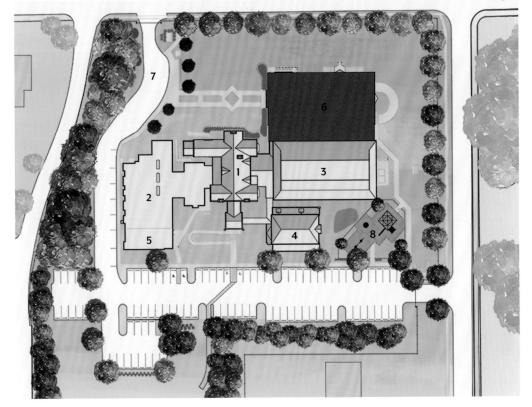

1 Historic Mansion
2 1974 High School Addition
3 1974 Gymnasium Addition
4 2010 Beit Midrash Addition
5 2018 Classroom Addition
6 New K-8 Lab School
7 Lab School Drop-off
8 Lab School Playground

YELLOW PONY FARM

Coatesville, Pennsylvania

ARCHER & BUCHANAN USED the gentle undulations of this Chester County site as a guide for placing the buildings and choreographing the drive sequence. The paddock fences read like contour lines and divide the 23-acres into different zones with the house on the high ground. The house is low slung with a series of repeating gable forms in various sizes that tie the composition together from all sides. The small, three-sided pool house with its open arches and stone chimney effectively anchors that end of the composition. The main residential block is a tight assemblage of similar shapes with the garage in between easing the scale transition.

Using the level plateau of the former cattle loafing sheds, a 12,500-square-foot indoor arena and six-stall barn was positioned in a hollow without spoiling the view from the residence on the hill above. Effectively camouflaged in natural, mossy colors, the large building nestles into the landscape. During both summer and winter months, it blends into conditions ranging from bright foliage and sunlight to foggy, grey days. By integrating daylighting from the roof and the perimeter into the arena and barn aisle, the lighting loads of the facility are reduced, thus creating a glare-free work environment for both horses and people. The complex is at home in its setting and reflects a highly disciplined arrangement of buildings with details in the vocabulary of the American shingle style, a familiar favorite for country and seaside houses at the turn of the century.

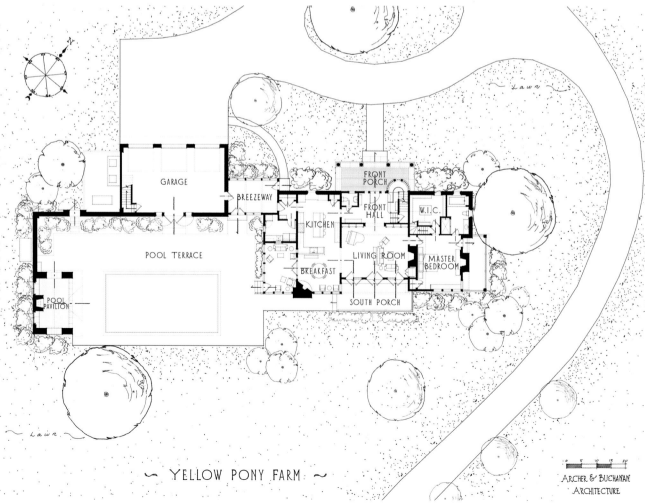

~ YELLOW PONY FARM ~

ARCHER & BUCHANAN
ARCHITECTURE

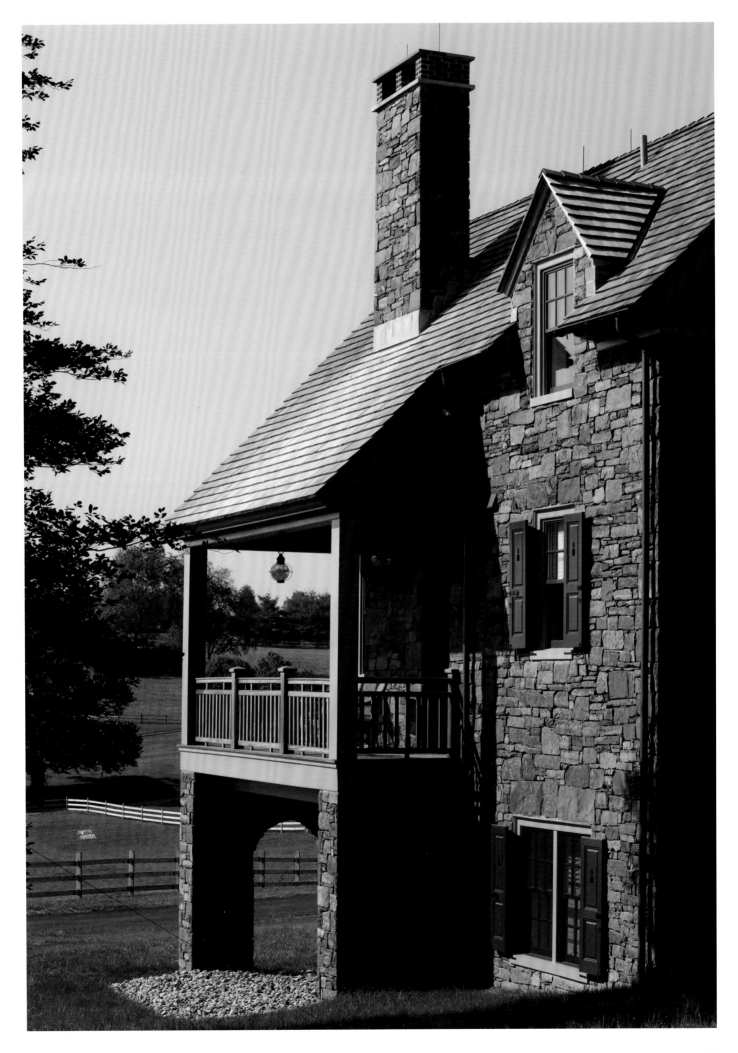

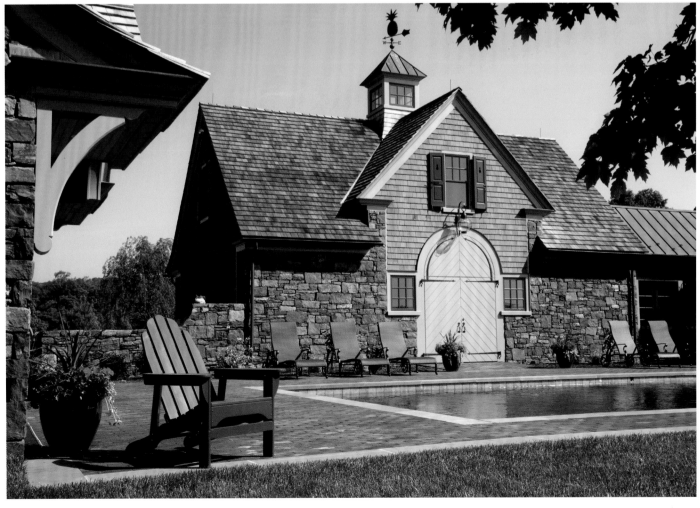

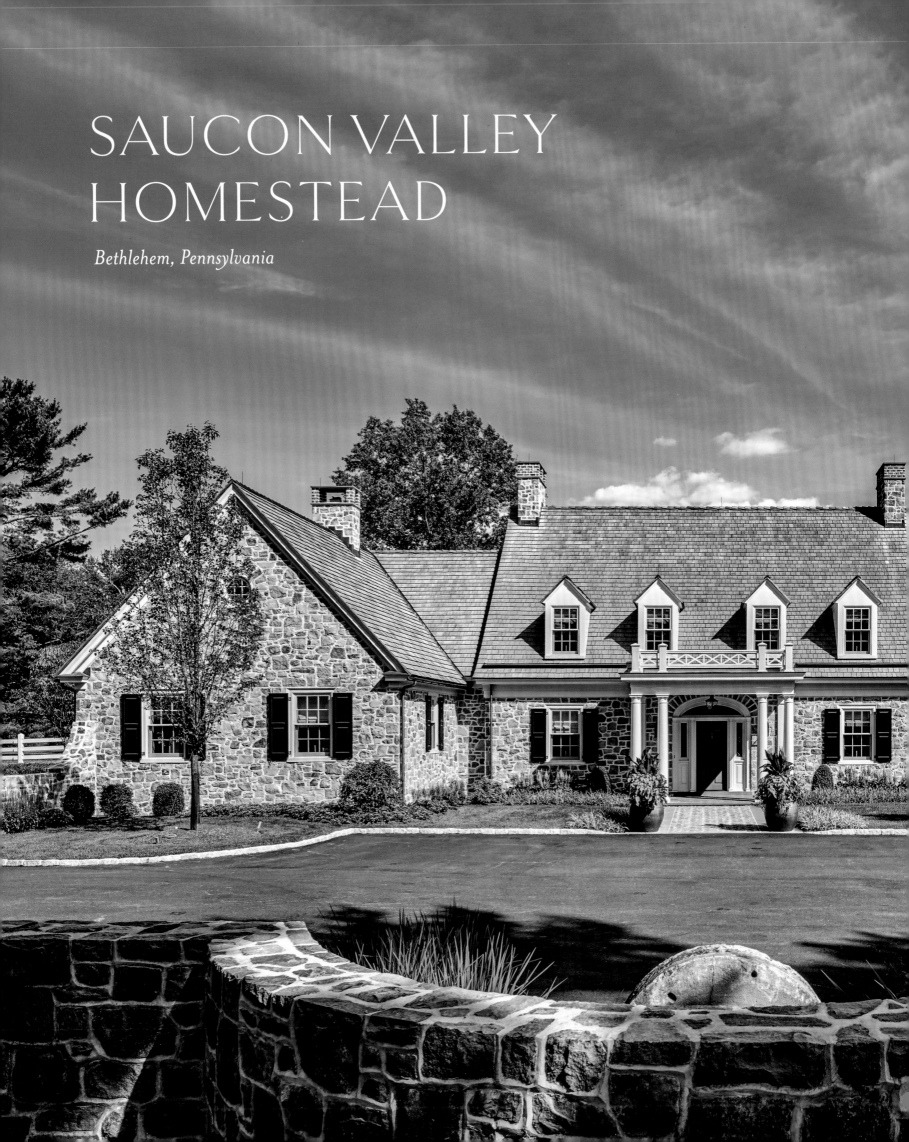

SAUCON VALLEY HOMESTEAD

Bethlehem, Pennsylvania

THE SAUCON VALLEY HOMESTEAD is set within scenic acreage earmarked by Bethlehem Steel Corporation in the 1950s for executive homes. Archer & Buchanan substantially renovated the existing house yet retained a shallow split-level arrangement for the primary living spaces. The addition of a party barn adjacent to the new pool and landscape elements create a unified entertainment and recreation area. From the outside, the additions and new buildings are integrated with the gardens to create outdoor rooms that complement the interior spaces. The master suite and garage establish two of the three walls of the entry court. The garage court provides additional parking and staging for activities in the barn, while the barn and covered terrace compose two sides of the pool court.

The generous proportions of the original dwelling enabled the center of the rear façade to appear as a full two-story, which helps to balance the size of the new stone-clad barn. The supplemental construction artfully combines local and English precedents in response to client aspirations and their program requirements. The inviting interior decoration by Tammy Connor features stylistic references that augment the architecture.

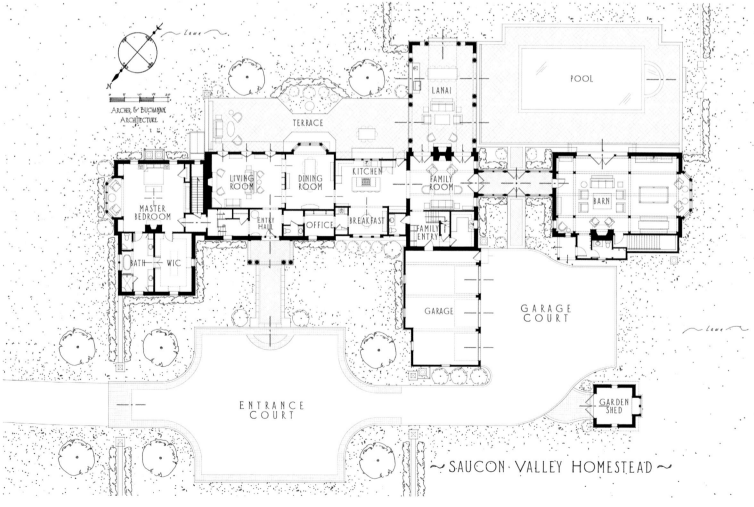

~ SAUCON VALLEY HOMESTEAD ~

NATURE

ENGAGEMENT WITH NATURE is an obvious necessity for architecture to harmonize within a setting. It is a choice, however, to understand and respect the natural and cultural character of a given location. It is a choice integral to the body of work by Archer & Buchanan, much of which can be found throughout the historic Mid-Atlantic region. The firm is intentional about creating structures that are sensitive to locale and offer a continuum. Designing with land stewardship as a priority guides the firm's approach to every commission; it accommodates change and adaptability and enhances the story behind each place.

The expansive views separated by mature trees on a rolling landscape provide the perfect setting for this house and its outbuildings.

The Hobbit House emerges out of a carefully curated landscape of nature and man–made construction.

Genius Loci, sometimes translated as "spirit of the place," philosophically describes the relationship of building to environment. For Archer & Buchanan, connection with a setting is largely independent of architectural style and is more about how nature and artifice coalesce to make memorable settings. Notably, many of the firm's projects have a combination of attributes that range from highly developed enclaves to swaths of untouched pastureland or dense forests. Looking at a few projects here demonstrates what the firm strives to bring to each landscape.

The Ardrossan Estate, twenty miles west of Philadelphia, offers several examples. Archer & Buchanan was responsible for projects on this former estate that responded to the beauty of extant fields and rolling terrain in different ways. One 6,000-square-foot residence is a single point in the larger overall landscape while the scenery is demarked by windbreaks and other boundary plantings remaining or restored. The house itself is a modest insertion with gracious porches marking the transition from building to nature. The architectural forms of the house and outbuildings have an ease in the setting and a sense of belonging.

Equally at home on the Ardrossan Estate are variations on the Pennsylvania farmhouse with programs that do not include barns or stables. They are based on the English manor house historically set in a landscape park adjacent to agricultural activities. When a project involves multiple structures and special purpose outbuildings, the technical program is also wedded to the aesthetic goals of the client. In the firm's farm or equestrian projects, nature takes on a multi-faceted role. Practical, functional needs have long guided the planning and architecture of farmsteads, but there is still room for artistic expression in the placement and detailing of the buildings and how they are set in the landscape. Cultivated or developed parcels, woodlands, wetlands, and undeveloped land all become part of the considered whole.

Nature can also be harnessed as part of a thematic vignette, assembled as a significant part of the setting. The Hobbit House was designed to be a container for a very special collection of art and objects. It is both a clue to what's inside and is distinct as the largest piece in the collection. The dry stone walls from another era, paths, and plantings surrounding the house add to the enchanting atmosphere, thoroughly transporting a visitor to the world of J. R. R. Tolkien.

Elements such as site walls built of native stone can likewise set the scene and become part of a new story. Walls and terraces that use the same or salvaged materials as the principal buildings reinforce the narrative of a place. At Mine Road Farm, the modest primary dwelling is linked to the other farm buildings on the site in this way. At the Lutyens-Inspired House, the garden and courtyard walls use the same stone and red roof tiles to reflect the vocabulary of the main house and create a strong connection between the site and the residence. The relationships between the architecture, the formal plantings, and the natural landscape recreate the classic English country house in central Pennsylvania.

Another project epitomizing those clear relationships is Fox Hill Farm near Unionville. Modeled on the English country house tradition, the sequenced balance of true nature and nature tamed underscores the architectural impact of the buildings. As microcosms of nature in the larger sense, formal gardens happily exist in large country or small urban settings. They may also have a different, more disciplined relationship to the architecture as they do at Fox Hill Farm.

By contrast to the two previously mentioned projects, the intimate Tea House pavilion at Wyndmoor exemplifies an entirely man-made environment. A small addition to an early-twentieth-century suburban residence, the surrounding landscape was designed to replicate a natural setting replete with a small watercourse and koi pond.

In sum, nature is more than a backdrop for the work of Archer & Buchanan. It is always part of the project program, reflects a love of the land, and makes a significant contribution to the design process. Whether a stunning country vista or intimate suburban setting, nature offers assets that are critical to the success of a realized project. It is an integration of *Genius Loci*, engaging the spirit of the place to inform the architecture, and using buildings to expand the meanings of the land.

Photography by: Tom Crane Photography, Archer & Buchanan Architecture

The native fieldstone used at Mine Road Farm reinforces regional building traditions and the story of a place.

The landscape features help the Tea House addition harmonize with the existing residence.

HONOR FARM

Kennett Square, Pennsylvania

CONVENTIONAL WISDOM SUGGESTS that the best building settings are on high ground with access to views and breezes. That point of view, however, overlooks the opportunities other locations may provide. The conservation easements on this property limited the buildable area to minimize impact of new construction in a carefully preserved landscape. The architects turned the limitation into an asset, taking advantage of the available contours to create privacy and a great entrance experience. From the winding drive, the chimney on the gable end is revealed first, then the full view of the front elevation appears just before arrival. The house and two small outbuildings are set in a shallow bowl surrounded by groves of trees and the rolling pastureland. The ensemble works with the land to shelter the home rather than aggrandize it.

The client's informal program inspired a compact building form with interiors that are spacious and flowing to accommodate entertaining. A family lumber business and interest in fine woodwork is reflected in the delicate, two-story, tightly curved stair. The walnut flooring and timber framing were salvaged from the Hartzell Propeller ("Built on Honor") lumber mills of Piqua, Ohio.

The pool house references springhouses found on many farmsteads in the area, and the pool looks like a spring-fed pond in the garden. The composition and the buildings turn an underappreciated parcel of land into a beloved environment.

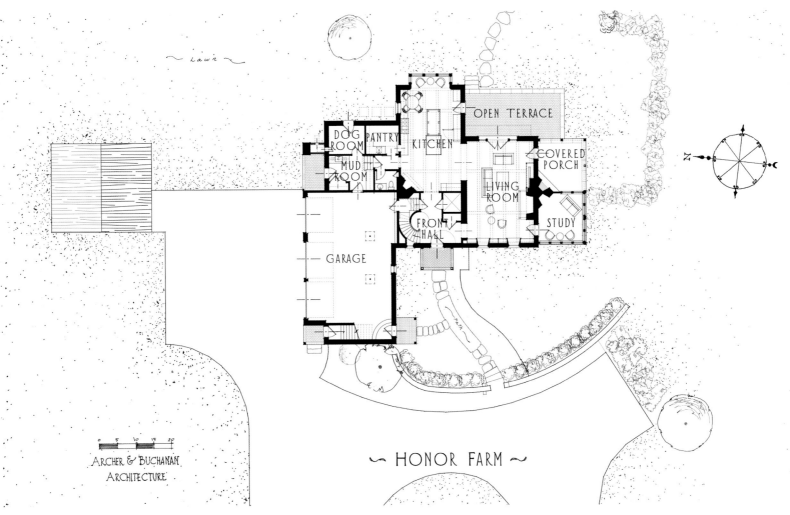

DOG ROOM
PANTRY
KITCHEN
OPEN TERRACE
MUD ROOM
COVERED PORCH
LIVING ROOM
FRONT HALL
STUDY
GARAGE

~ Lawn ~

~ HONOR FARM ~

ASIAN-INSPIRED RESIDENCE

llanova, Pennsylvania

IN 1965, THE PREVIOUS OWNERS of this property assembled a home and garden which completely evoked a Japanese country residence. While the beautifully maintained garden had approached its mature expression, the home had deteriorated beyond repair. Nonetheless, the Japanese sensibility matched the new owners' interest in Asian philosophies so, with Archer & Buchanan, they set about creating a new house inspired by the property.

The design for the new 6,000-square-foot house creates serene relationships between the interior rooms and exterior landscaping. The plan loosely conforms to the former layout and accords views from the major rooms into an internal courtyard while the first-floor master suite looks out to a private garden. A dramatic Great Room is the focal point of the house with its large scale, open plan, and panoramic views. Dark timber construction contrasts against bright walls of plaster or glass in this double height space and Balinese influences are evident in the decoratively cut timber posts, beams, and trusses. Bedroom suites for the children are on the second floor and radiate around a towering central atrium with a cupola.

On the exterior, deep overhanging eaves have stained timber brackets and embellished rafter tails. The front porch, trellis walkway, and pool house interpret at different scales the decorative timber post and beam details of the Great Room interior. At the south porch, the dry-laid ashlar stone wraps from exterior to interior, blurring the distinctions between outside and inside. Landscape Architect, Joe Blandy, used many existing garden features while incorporating new Japanese design elements and details. The result, while shaped by the original house and property, is an utterly unique home that reflects the tranquility and openness of its Asian influences.

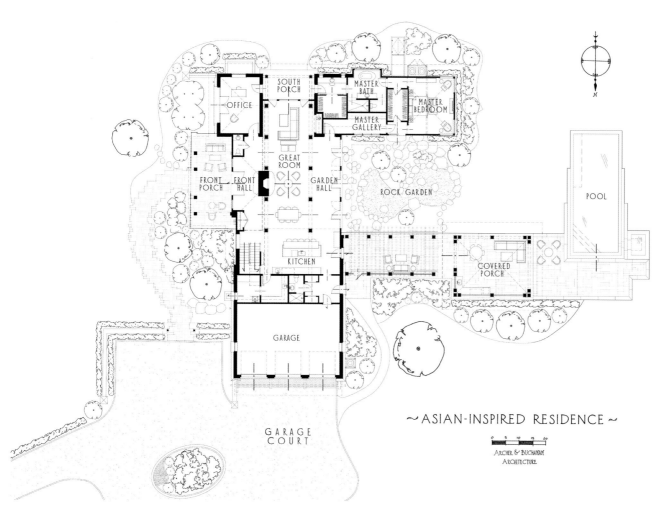

~ASIAN-INSPIRED RESIDENCE ~

ARCHER & BUCHANAN
ARCHITECTURE

BURROWS RUN

Centreville, Delaware

BURROWS RUN WAS DESIGNED by R. Brognard Okie in 1939 for Nicholas and Genevieve (Bunny) du Pont. Okie had been a favored architect of the du Ponts, designing their homes in the Brandywine Valley and its environs. This house, previously known as "Ridgely," was smaller and less formal than Okie's typical designs for the family, but otherwise displayed his signature details and imaginative composition of masses.

The current generation called in Archer & Buchanan to preserve the original character of Okie's vision, eliminate awkward interventions, and provide a contemporary reworking of the plan to meet current needs. The evolution of lifestyles absent staff meant the kitchen in this house could be closer to the view and integrated with the family room. To accomplish this, the 70s era solarium was replaced. A larger, simplified Master Suite was created out of smaller rooms and an elevator was discretely added into the plan.

To ensure the next century of family use and appreciation, the Ludowici clay tile roofing was removed and re-laid with new underpinnings. Okie's trademark field stone and robust millwork were also restored to their original specifications.

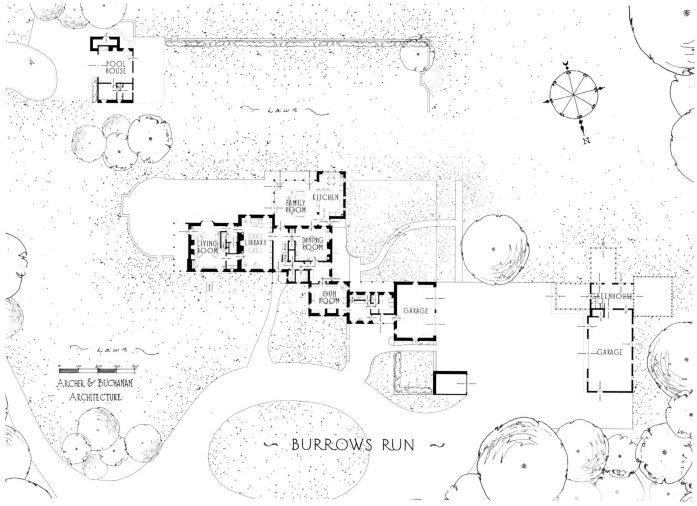

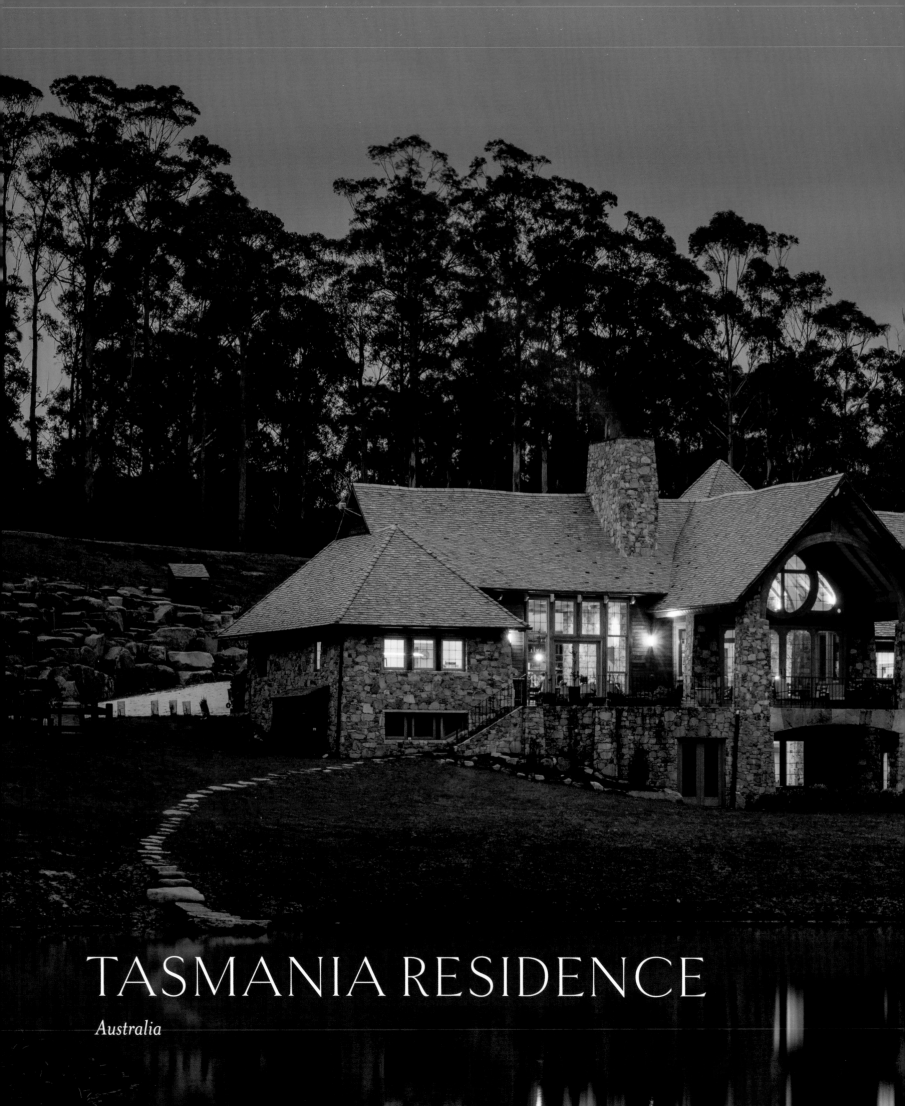

TASMANIA RESIDENCE

Australia

DESIGNING A NEW RESIDENCE on the Australian island province of Tasmania provided an unusual opportunity to work with Arts & Crafts architectural styles as conveyed in the writing of J. R. R. Tolkien. Construction techniques fused old world design traditions with local resources and trades. The realized 6,500-square-foot heavy timber dwelling looks toward Sleeping Beauty Mountain and brings the features of an English cottage to the wilderness setting where environmental sustainability is both a goal and a requirement.

Designing for water and energy conservation are key regional concerns, addressed by groundwater source heat pumps, photovoltaics, rainwater harvesting, and use of sustainably sourced construction materials. In addition to bringing green design techniques to the project, the process and logistics relied on the technologies of video conferencing and 3D digital presentations between the clients, builders, and architects who were separated halfway around the globe.

The completed building shows that the surrounding geography enriched the outcome as did the rigorous planning, design, and integration of materiality consistent with the body of work from Archer & Buchanan.

VILLANOVA RESIDENCE

Villanova, Pennsylvania

THIS HOUSE BY ARCHER & BUCHANAN embodies the values that made R. Brognard Okie's architecture so progressive. The firm's design demonstrates how abstract architectural concepts combined with deft handling of traditional design motifs can produce a unique result.

Situated on fourteen acres subdivided from the former 800-acre Ardrossan Estate, the plan of the house was restricted by conservation easements and other architectural controls. The clients had an interest in Pennsylvania stone farmhouses, but not a typical center hall Colonial. They wanted their house to reflect a more informal lifestyle, make the most of sensational views, and echo traditional detailing typified by surviving farm buildings.

As the long entrance drive curves down, the four-bay stone Colonial comes into view. On closer examination, familiar imagery used in innovative ways become evident. The right hand bay for example, has a slightly different window spacing and a seam in the stone suggesting that it might be from a different construction phase, thus shifting the center of visual gravity to the wide front door. On the left, the lower wing with offset windows hints at a stair, yet only upon passing through the front door is the true plan revealed. The center hall is turned sideways as a grand promenade, affording access to all of the major rooms on the first floor. Three elliptical arches open to the sunken living room while the light filled stair is at one end of the hall. The deep blue Butler's Pantry anchors the other end and leads to the kitchen and less formal family spaces.

In harmony with the history of its surroundings, this house exemplifies vitality in traditional design. One hundred years ago, Colonial Revival was about the rediscovery of an ancestral language. Adaptation to twenty-first-century practicalities and building technologies give new currency to the applied style. The result renders comfort in the familiar and delight in the unexpected.

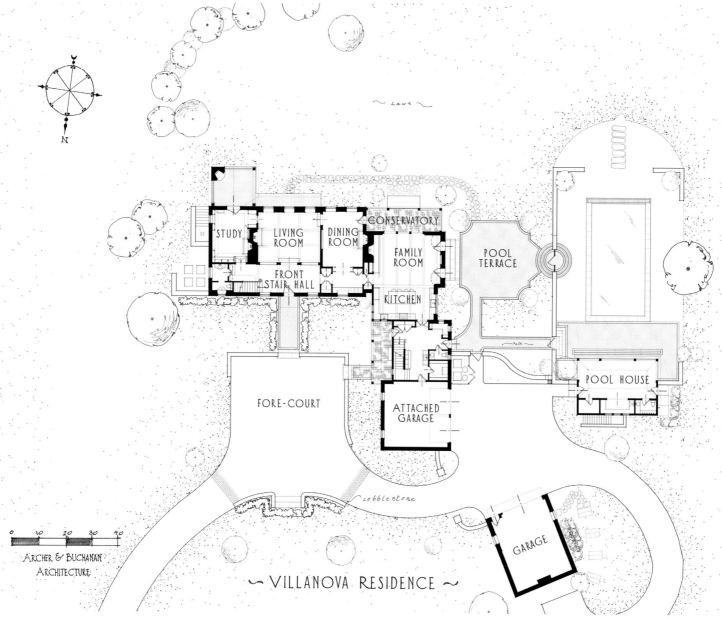

STUDY

LIVING ROOM

DINING ROOM

CONSERVATORY

FAMILY ROOM

POOL TERRACE

FRONT STAIR HALL

KITCHEN

POOL HOUSE

FORE-COURT

ATTACHED GARAGE

GARAGE

~ Lawn ~

~ Path ~

cobblestone

ARCHER & BUCHANAN ARCHITECTURE

0 10 20 30 40

~ VILLANOVA RESIDENCE ~

LENFEST CENTER

Coatesville, Pennsylvania

THE LENFEST MANAGEMENT and Preserve Center serves a dual purpose. It houses operational support for the 1,383-acre Cheslen Preserve and is a facility for public outreach events. The structure is based on the traditional bank barn arrangement with at-grade access on two levels. The design provides a minimal footprint on the landscape while offering separate entry to land preserve activities and public use of the facility. The lower level is dedicated to Preserve maintenance, including vehicular and equipment service areas and material and supply storage. The public functions are on the main level and include an orientation lobby, meeting room, offices, catering kitchen, and restrooms. An open-air pavilion supports outdoor events and features fireplaces, publicly accessible restrooms, and scenic views. Inspired by the bucolic rural setting, the facility embodies the functional and timeless beauty of Chester County agrarian architecture through its use of materials, details, and forms.

Principal in Charge: Dan Russoniello, AIA, LEED AP

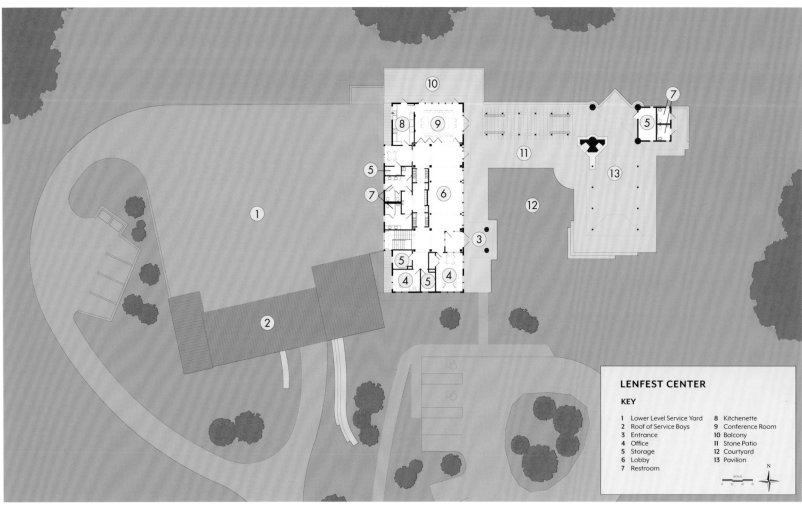

LENFEST CENTER

KEY

1	Lower Level Service Yard	8	Kitchenette
2	Roof of Service Bays	9	Conference Room
3	Entrance	10	Balcony
4	Office	11	Stone Patio
5	Storage	12	Courtyard
6	Lobby	13	Pavilion
7	Restroom		

CONTEXT

ARCHITECTURAL CONTEXT RELATES to time, place, history, and culture. For buildings, context most often refers to a physical setting and includes both the natural and man-made features. The context of time is more nuanced and may reference a particular period, which in turn establishes styles of design, types of construction, and the historical or cultural heritage of a particular community. History indelibly records our culture, stories, norms, events, priorities, and traditions. Architecture is a physical manifestation that charts our history. Buildings provide the context that the future inherits, which is what gives architecture meaning.

*Distinctive detailing inspired by
R. Brognard Okie imbues this
space with historic context.*

*Okie-based woodworking details
are adapted to new programs
throughout the building.*

The purposeful use and understanding of contextual cues is a key element in the work of Archer & Buchanan. Consideration of context sets up the narratives that inform the design and experience of a given project; possibilities are created that imbue definition and interest. Merging traditional forms, materials, and building methods with contemporary design and technologies, the firm brings appreciation of history to their work, allowing each project to contribute to the ever evolving context of building in southeastern Pennsylvania. To fully appreciate the firm's body of work, it is interesting to consider the historical and geographical forces inherent to this specific region.

In the mid-seventeenth century, European settlers arrived in the middle Atlantic colonies where they encountered climate and landforms similar to their homeland. Design principles and traditions were adapted and expressed through locally available building materials. In most of the rural areas, stone would dominate, while brick was more prevalent in cities and towns. By the mid-eighteenth century, a degree of uniformity rendered the "Pennsylvania Farmhouse" as a recognized regional building type.

Proximity to Philadelphia is also relevant as the city's sophisticated trade guilds gave rise to architecture as a profession. By the late 1800s and early 1900s, accomplished young firms were flourishing, creating residences and civic work that influenced the development of a strong regional context. At the same time, the surrounding rural areas benefited from new sources of materials and a dissemination of new design thinking.

Later, the fabled suburban development along Pennsylvania Railroad's Main Line included residential design by distinguished architects such as William Price and R. Brognard Okie. Today, Archer & Buchanan strives to further the architectural and contextual legacy of these late-nineteenth-century architects and others. Not only has the firm sensitively undertaken projects incorporating buildings by these masters; the new work continues a contextual tradition, adds to the narrative, and extends use and enjoyment of the buildings.

In fact, although separated by 100 years, Okie and Archer & Buchanan share a similar approach to design, responding to a client's program with familiar forms utilized in an unexpected manner. Deeply rooted to context, the finished projects are at once picturesque but also rigorous in how each part supports the whole. In Archer & Buchanan's involvement with significant existing Okie works like Bryn Coed, for instance, the alterations and additions range from minor changes to new construction that is clearly an addition, but all reinforce the architecture of the original building. While Archer & Buchanan always considers and integrates antecedents, several other projects stand out as clear examples of how overlapping criteria inform the design. With no set formula, it is up to the designer to evaluate the contextual forces of time, place, history, and culture to develop a balanced response.

The milieu of the Mill Creek House addition, shown on the opening page of this essay (p. 94), was unusual for the Main Line. Set alongside a stream surrounded by a mature landscape, the original 40-year-old contemporary house made quite a statement. Subtle changes update the existing building envelope without dramatically changing its appearance. Larger interventions, however, include a timber-framed, screened-in aviary. Although the aviary follows the basic forms of the existing building, it uses a bold color palette in visible contrast rather than simply relying on building details that clearly show it as new construction.

In rural Unionville, a small eighteenth-century tenant farmhouse with an 1888 bank barn offered the opportunity to execute new work in contrast to the original buildings. The response skillfully incorporates modern movement glass walls and flat roofs while using a traditional form to connect the barn to the small farmhouse. In this example, contextual design blends design periods within a historic landscape yet retains the integrity of the original structures.

In a more suburban setting along the Main Line, a pre-war, Cotswold-style home features a new addition that mines the same vernacular sources as the original building. The roof profiles, dramatic double-height bay window, and other architectural features owe a debt to Sir Edwin Lutyens and his brilliant twentieth-century work in England that influenced countless buildings on both sides of the Atlantic. The extension, which incorporates a new family room, screened porch, and adjacent outdoor terraces, injects new life into a conservative, quiet building in the best way. In this example, Archer & Buchanan complements the existing structure with additions that enhance livability as well as the overall form.

Rural landscapes with a variety of structures contain many contextual opportunities.

The inventive forms in English country houses provide a range of inspiration for contemporary application.

New construction in historic districts can add to the visual quality through thoughtful use of traditional design motifs.

The new addition to the Kohelet Yeshiva Lab School responds to the existing architecture by respecting the scale and materials of the original building.

Recently, zoning and planning codes have attempted to address context and how regulations can preserve character defining features in town and rural settings. Infill buildings that do not include commercial storefronts are a Main Street design challenge. In the railroad suburb of Bryn Mawr on Philadelphia's Main Line, Archer & Buchanan referenced existing early-twentieth-century retail buildings for a redevelopment project. The new building reinforces the traditional streetwall with ground floor retail and apartments above. The overall organization and variety of window openings at the sidewalk level relate to the town's context for commercial architecture. The use of ornamental brick patterns on the principal façade is a nod to the other mixed-use buildings along the main street.

The planning for the expansion of the Kohelet Yeshiva Lab School likewise required navigating a number of contexts. The new building contributes a much-needed facility to the campus, relates to the extant buildings, and provides a connection to the community at an important street intersection. The design is clearly institutional while the exterior materials relate to the core building of the school, a large turn-of-the-century stone manor house with several later additions. Archer & Buchanan exposed as much of the original house as possible while allowing the new building to have its own presence.

The convergence of time, the culture and history of a place, the physical landscape, and the memories associated with it create a multilayered context. A client's aspirations and requirements are met through study and interpretation of the layers. For every commission, whether new construction, an addition, or restoration, Archer & Buchanan assembles nimble architectural responses that result in places that seem inevitable not just for the client, but for the surrounding community and environment.

Photography by: Archer & Buchanan Architecture, Angle Eye Photography,
Tom Crane Photography, Halkin/Mason Photography

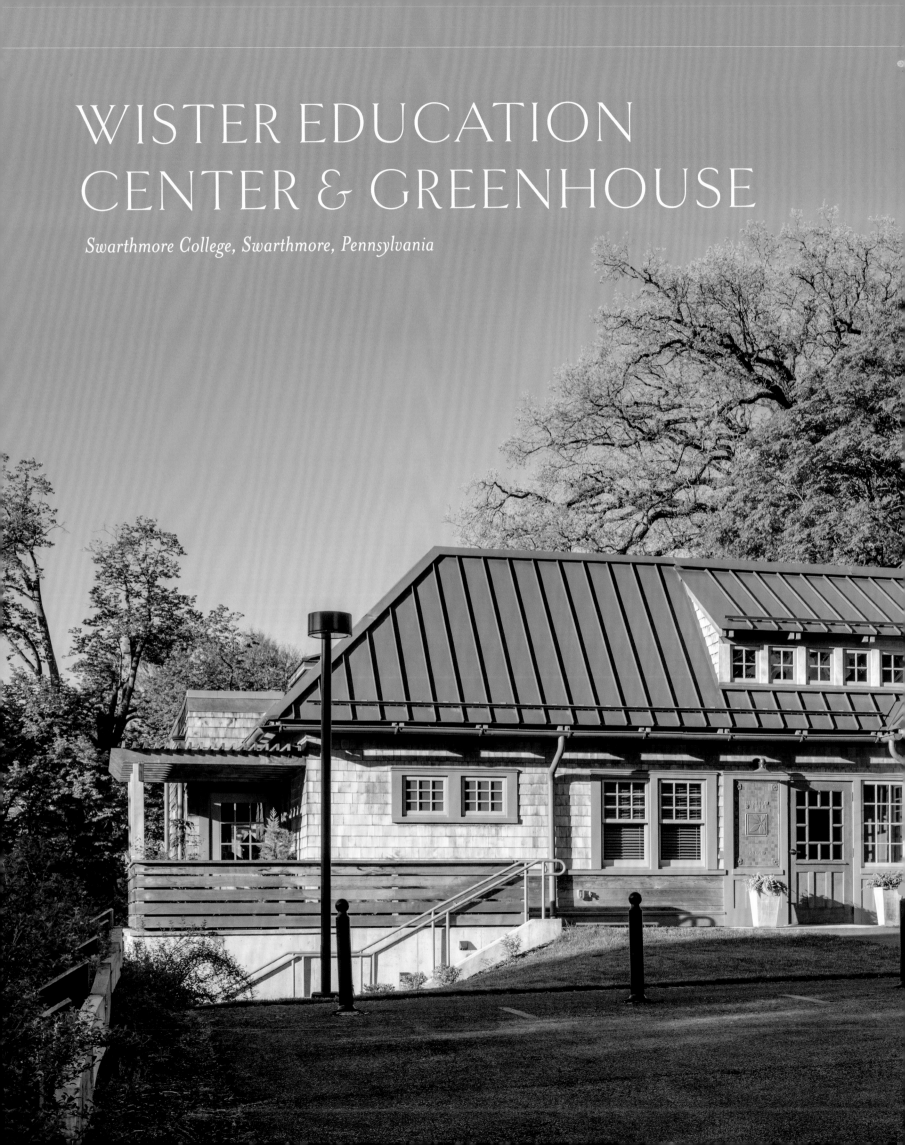

WISTER EDUCATION CENTER & GREENHOUSE

Swarthmore College, Swarthmore, Pennsylvania

LOCATED IN THE SCOTT ARBORETUM at the main entrance to Swarthmore College, the Wister Education Center and Greenhouse serves the staff and volunteers of the arboretum, promotes their mission "for the encouragement of horticulture in its broadest sense," and supports the accredited and nationally-renowned arboretum in maintaining its reputation for being, "the most beautiful college campus in America." A LEED Gold certified facility, the 5,200-square-foot building includes a 2,400-square-foot greenhouse with individual chambers dedicated to plant propagation, overwintering, cultivation, and display, and a workroom for potting, soil mixing, and other greenhouse-related activities. The building also houses a classroom, reception area, kitchen, and office and service space.

The scale of the building is compatible to the turn-of-the-century cottage which serves as the administrative center for the arboretum and the forms and colors of the new building blend with the plantings of the site. The result achieves its intended goals by providing a state-of-the-art greenhouse, durable and flexible work areas, and well-planned public spaces, but also embodies the design relationships of building to site, greenhouse to sunlight, inside to outside, and architecture to landscape.

Principal in Charge: Dan Russoniello, AIA, LEED AP

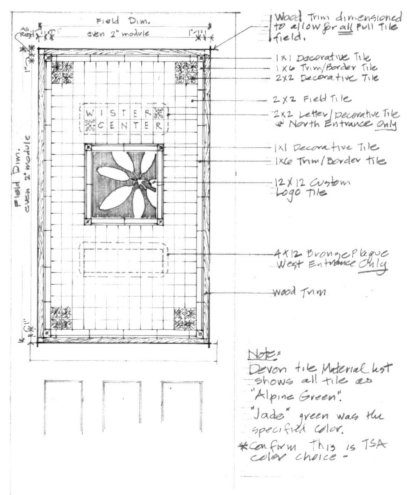

Field Dim.
even 2" module

Field Dim. even 2" module

W I S T E R
CENTER

Wood Trim dimensioned to allow for all full Tile field.

1×1 Decorative Tile
1×6 Trim/Border Tile
2×2 Decorative Tile

2×2 Field Tile

2×2 Letter/Decorative Tile @ North Entrance Only

1×1 Decorative Tile
1×6 Trim/Border tile

12×12 Custom Logo Tile

4×12 Bronze Plaque West Entrance Only

Wood Trim

Note:
Devon tile Material list shows all tile as "Alpine Green".

"Jade" green was the specified color.

*Confirm this is TSA color choice—

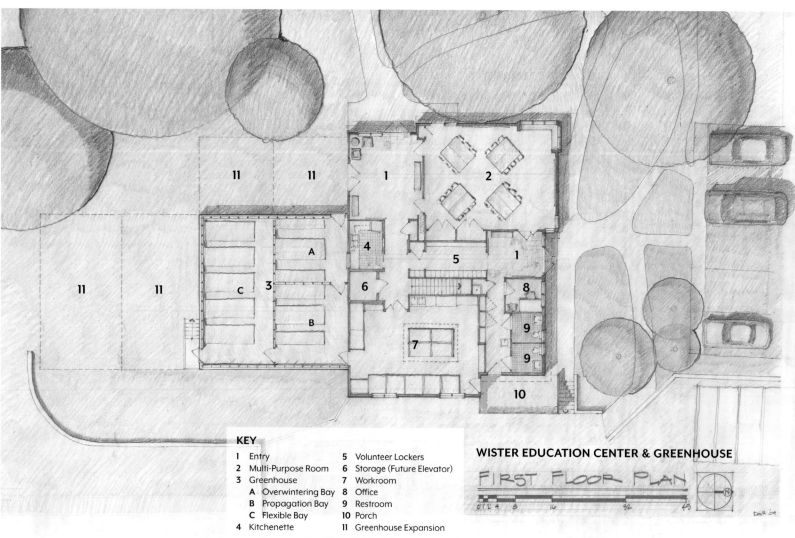

KEY

1 Entry
2 Multi-Purpose Room
3 Greenhouse
  A Overwintering Bay
  B Propagation Bay
  C Flexible Bay
4 Kitchenette

5 Volunteer Lockers
6 Storage (Future Elevator)
7 Workroom
8 Office
9 Restroom
10 Porch
11 Greenhouse Expansion

WISTER EDUCATION CENTER & GREENHOUSE

FIRST FLOOR PLAN

CLOCKTOWER FARM

West Chester, Pennsylvania

IN SPITE OF ENCROACHING SUBURBIA, the house at Clocktower Farm survived the late-nineteenth-century gentrification of area farmsteads. The original early-nineteenth-century house was modernized in the 1880s with new service areas and interiors reflecting the fashion of the era and over a hundred years later, the house, a barn, and the wonderful clock tower (which originally held a water tank) miraculously remained on a grassy sloped site bounded by mature trees.

The substantial new addition by Archer & Buchanan is artfully incorporated into the existing structure with varying shapes and details derived from the original house. The approach from the road emphasizes the tower and the primary façades. Inside, the front rooms and stair hall have been restored and retain extant mantelpieces and decorative details. These rooms open into the bright new kitchen and great room that expand out to the porches and lawn beyond. The house is complemented by extensive landscaping including a sunken garden, pool, and pool house. The barn has been renovated as an event venue.

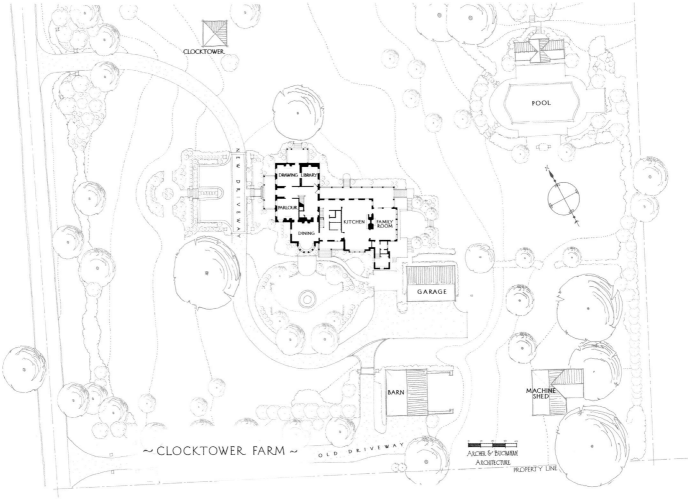

CLOCKTOWER

POOL

NEW DRIVEWAY

DRAWING | LIBRARY
PARLOUR
DINING | KITCHEN | FAMILY ROOM

GARAGE

BARN

MACHINE SHED

~ CLOCKTOWER FARM ~ OLD DRIVEWAY

ARCHER & BUCHANAN ARCHITECTURE

PROPERTY LINE

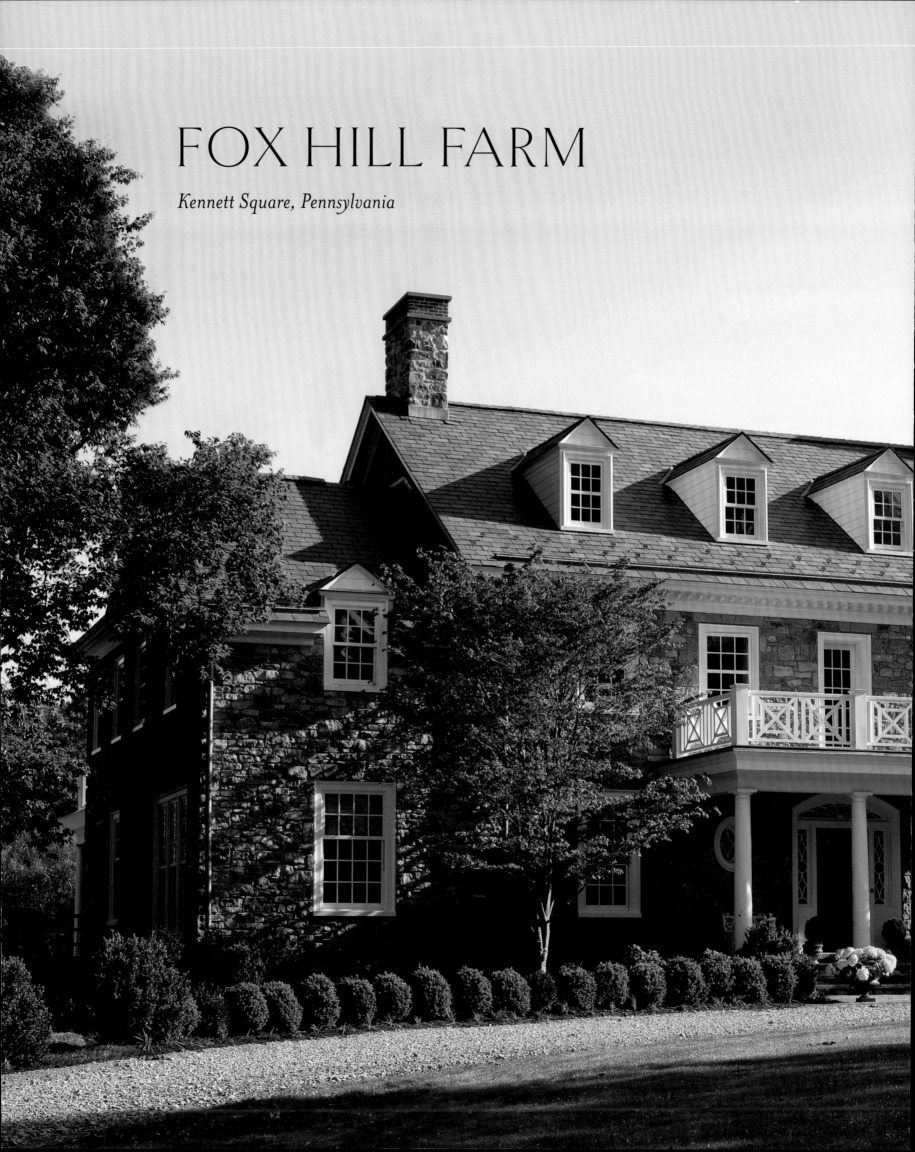

FOX HILL FARM

Kennett Square, Pennsylvania

THE FOX HILL FARM RESIDENCE is an entirely new replacement of an earlier house. It is sited directly on the former footprint to leave the existing legacy arboretum intact. Designed sympathetically and in concert with its surroundings, the new house is often mistaken for the home built 90 years earlier. The new structure, however, addresses the contemporary needs of a large family with ample living spaces that open to the gardens, pond, and fields. The sense of place comes from architecture at home in the historical context of the area. That feeling is reinforced by the use of traditional materials including the architectural salvage of flooring, mantels, doors, and hardware from older structures. The exterior and interior details impart an easy formality that is appropriate to the country setting.

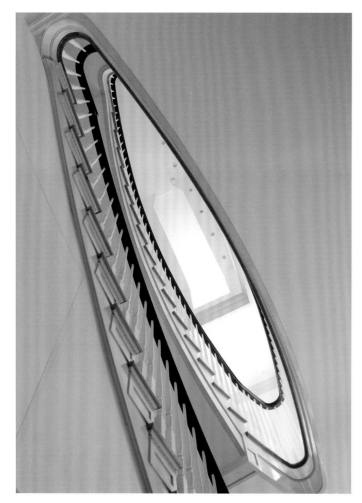

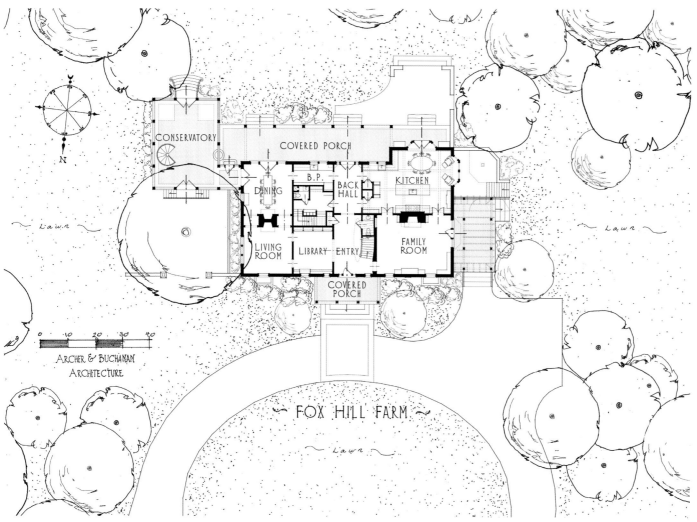

ARCHER & BUCHANAN
ARCHITECTURE

CONSERVATORY

COVERED PORCH

DINING

B.P.

BACK HALL

KITCHEN

LIVING ROOM

LIBRARY

ENTRY

FAMILY ROOM

COVERED PORCH

~ FOX HILL FARM ~

LUTYENS-INSPIRED RESIDENCE

Lewisburg, Pennsylvania

DURING HIS LONG CAREER, the English architect Sir Edwin Lutyens (1869-1944) was known for imaginative adaptations of English country and classical styles. His architecture remains a great inspiration, but as a deeply personal expression, difficult to adapt. This residence in Lewisburg has just the right setting for a building inspired by a master of the rural vernacular. The rolling contours, ponds, and copses of trees evoke the idyllic landscape of the Cotswolds. Into this setting, Archer & Buchanan reinterprets the romantic architecture of pastoral England in brick, half-timber, and clay roofing tiles.

A formal court and entry define the front with a roofscape in red tile that progresses from a primary shape over the core of the house to a variegated assembly of gables and carefully executed details. The enclosure created by the forecourt flows into a series of open and covered porches with sweeping views of the provincial countryside.

The building plan features regularly spaced brick piers and arches to add discipline and organization to the layout, separating the formal rooms from the everyday living spaces. Lutyens designed his country homes with a balance of formality and playfulness to provide reprieve from the city. This twenty-first-century country house expresses the same intent.

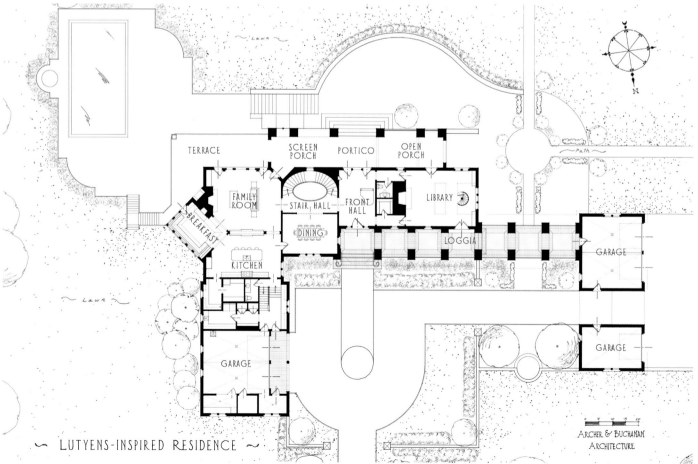

~ LUTYENS-INSPIRED RESIDENCE ~

ARCHER & BUCHANAN
ARCHITECTURE

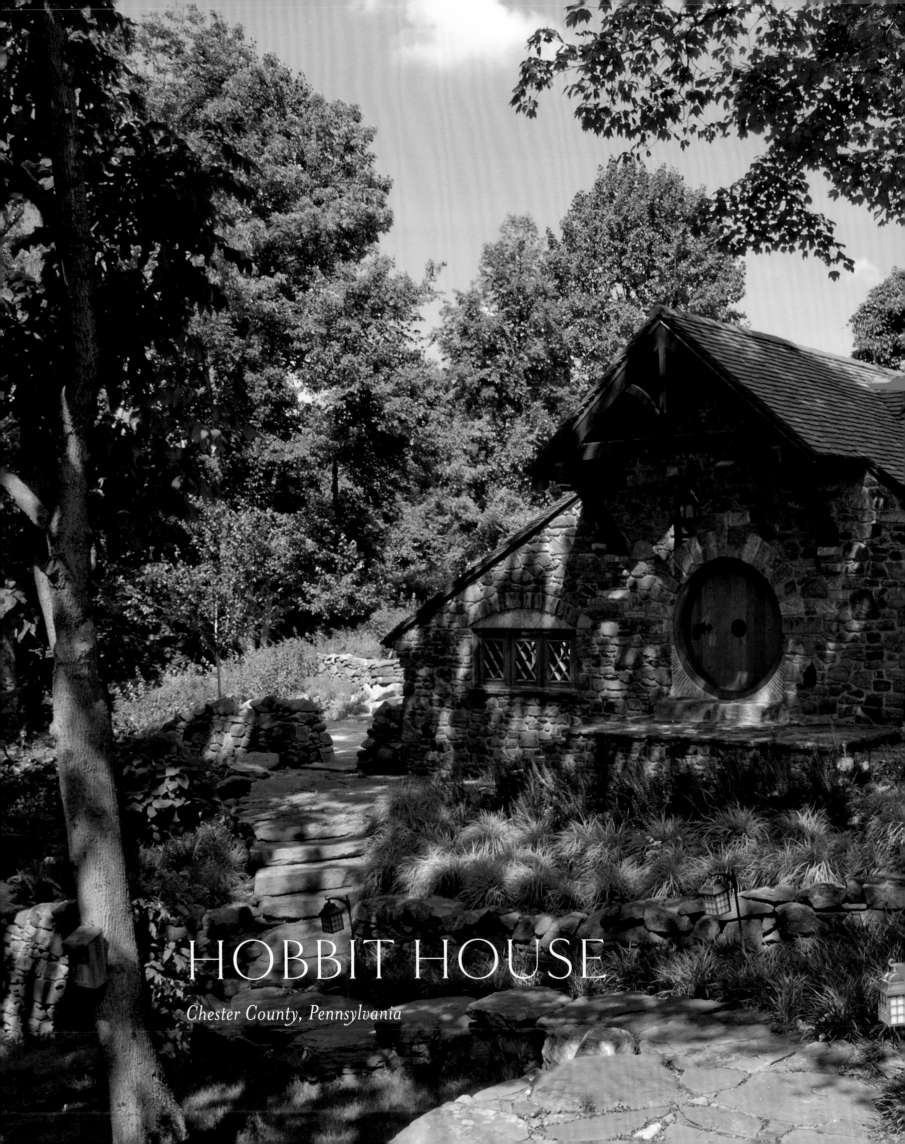

HOBBIT HOUSE

Chester County, Pennsylvania

J. R. R. TOLKIEN CREATED a magical fantasy world in Middle-earth as the setting for his stories. On a wooded site in Chester County, Archer & Buchanan created an enchanting stone house for a collector of materials and artifacts related to Tolkien's work, which thoroughly evokes Hobbit homes in The Shire. The landscape, exterior, and interior create a transportive other world, perfectly suited for the collection and quiet sanctuary.

The small building draws its inspiration directly from the descriptive language of the literature, and although it is sited close to the owner's residence, it feels far away. The whimsical design is masterfully executed and fabricated. A standout exterior detail is the Butterfly Window, a circle in a semicircle with the operating parts hinged from the center, like wings. Clever details of wood and metal are featured in the door openings, exposed structure, and custom light fixtures. The exterior stonework moors the building to the site under a flowing roof of handmade clay tiles. The front of the house is built into an eighteenth-century dry stone wall that runs through the property. Salvaged stone from the same wall completes the house to great effect.

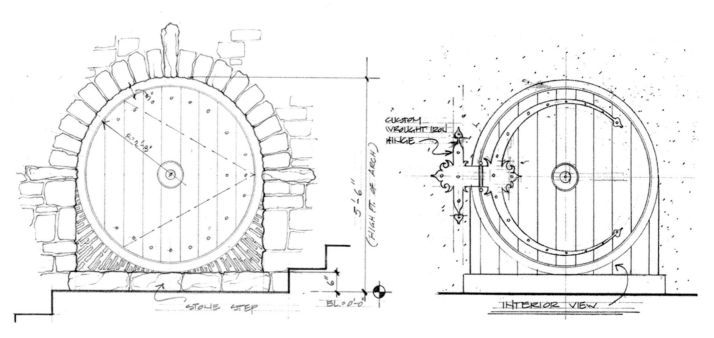

ROUND DOOR DETAIL

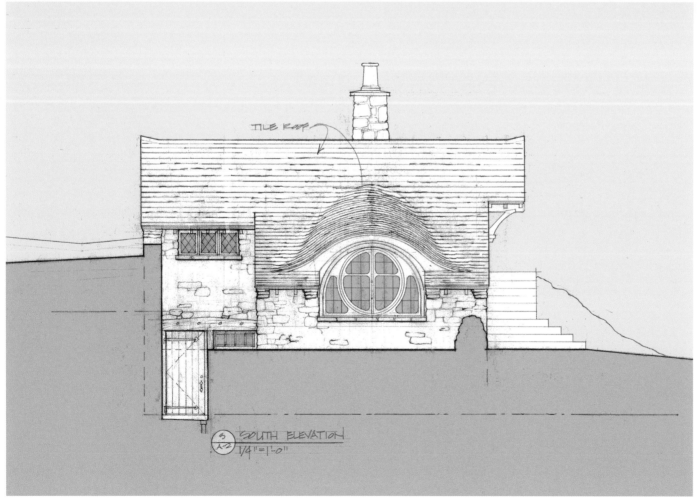

TILE ROOF

⑤ SOUTH ELEVATION
1/4"=1'-0"

MOMENTS

WHAT IS THE DIFFERENCE BETWEEN a moment in architecture and the full story? Is it a chapter, a quotation, or a summary? In short, a moment unites qualities of all three to reference the completeness of a project. Moments are one of the defining characteristics of a disciplined design process in the ways they fulfill expectations. A moment is both the spark that ignites a project and a distillation of the big picture.

The architecture of Archer & Buchanan is defined by moments. Difficult to achieve consistently, moments truly separate exceptional design from the commonplace, offering delight in overt or subtle ways. According to Vitruvius, the first century BCE Roman architect and engineer, the virtues of architecture are *Utilitas, Firmitatis, Venustatis*. Commodity, Firmness, and Delight.

The inventive, multi–story bay window at Speakman Hill is revealed when the house is seen from the rear.

The pool pavilion at Yellow Pony Farm is a distillation of the design themes represented in the main house.

Distinctive details and craftsmanship define the entrance hall at Home Bred Farm.

It might be said that Delight comes from the art of architecture. It is the aspect that elevates architecture into a sensory experience. Delight comes from the moments that provoke engagement from those experiencing the buildings and setting. A project can have more than one moment. Moments can build to a common climax or be episodic. Often, they relate to the order in which experiences of a place unfold, either for the first time or on an ongoing basis. A moment gives pause for reflecting how pieces connect to the whole.

The impact of moments is not limited to objects or forms, but also feelings and the memories they evoke. Feelings can include a sense of welcoming embrace, drama through light and shadow, or serenity through color or sound. The reaction to a moment may evolve over time with familiarity, but it never goes away. A glimpse into several of Archer & Buchanan's commissions follow to demonstrate diverse moments and the delight they conjure.

The residence at Speakman Hill Farm references the brick Colonial-era prototypes in southern Chester County. The overall massing and expected details such as the pent eaves are little preparation for the multi-story semi-circular bay window at the rear elevation, a gesture that introduces new forms in an inventive, yet cohesive manner. It is not visible from the approach, but occurs where the sloping site adds a full story to the wall height. The curved walls and especially the curved window sashes are a delightful adaptation of traditional forms.

The ensemble planning at Yellow Pony Farm illustrates how a singular component representing the larger work can be used compellingly. In this case, the roofed open-air pool pavilion, seen at a distance on the approach to the building group, displays the most important architectural elements and details from the residence and garage. First seen as a completely separate structure, the pavilion's oversized chimney and arches in the gable ends repeat some of the basic geometry established on the main structures, but in a simplified fashion. On closer view, refined details come to the fore, such as the bracketed curved eaves, and then, emerging from the shadows, an arched fireplace. This is a moment that broadens as the viewer's distance diminishes.

At Home Bred Farm, the entrance establishes a wonderful opening moment. The front doors and entry hall give the impression that an existing barn has been converted to a new timber-framed residence. The oversized doors, brick floor, and hay loft ladder hint at the details that occur within the main part of the house. This moment of entry captures the imagination and creates an expectation of distinctive materials and craftsmanship. Indeed, the custom metalwork in hardware and fittings and combinations of masonry and timber achieve a level of refinement beyond a working barn conversion. Crossing the threshold also heightens spatial awareness as the entry transitions to the volumes of the stair and great hall.

The Wister Education Center in the Scott Arboretum provides an example of a moment not fully revealed on first glance. The building is deceptively simple in accord with the Quaker values of the institution and does not upstage the landscape, the real star of the show. The strong geometry of the roof shapes and building mass have some finer elements that link it to other buildings in the campus setting. The projected corner bay uses the same components as the rest of the exterior envelope, but it draws attention with its placement and subtle shifts in plane, cantilevering out from the wall foundations. A simple gesture perhaps, but one that becomes clear in the main classroom space of the building. Inside, the bay becomes an intimate seating area within a large space, offering usability for small groups or impromptu meetings. The moment is reinforced by detailing that relates to the floating nature of the exterior form.

Finally, a moment may be part of a project that is extra special in and of itself. Two examples show a range in this type of expression. First, the Butler's Pantry in the Villanova Residence features woodwork and use of color indicative of motives found throughout the house, but here those aspects are amplified. The glass fronts and lighting display shimmering crystal and china against the rich, deep blue of the room. A starry sky on the ceiling adds another note of glitter. Passing through the Butler's Pantry manifests the connections and contrasts between the formal entrance hall and the casual kitchen and its supporting spaces.

Secondly, a different type of moment arises when a building exterior sets up a different expectation other than what is experienced inside. The house at Big Bend had conservation easements that strictly limited alterations to its exterior. The plain Pennsylvania farmhouse thus belies the elegant new interior created for the next generation of occupants. A dazzling new stair is the focal point of the renovation. To maximize impact, Archer & Buchanan introduce architectural elements for the stair and interior inspired by the sophisticated work of John Soane in Britain and Benjamin Henry Latrobe in America in the early-nineteenth century. The deliberate choice of refined detailing to draw attention to the spatial geometry is pure delight. This moment kindles a dialogue between the simplicity of the original farmhouse and the sophistication of the new interiors.

Over two thousand years ago, Vitruvius identified moments—of discovery and enchantment—as a crucial component for architecture. Moments stimulate the senses and become memorable. They also have the power to remain fresh. As part of an exterior or site design, a moment can be a public delight. Inside, they are a special gift. The moments cited above are a small sampling of the richness in design and the completeness of execution that typify the work of Archer & Buchanan.

Photography by: Jim Graham Photography, Archer & Buchanan Architecture,
Tom Crane Photography, Arcaid Images / Alamy Stock Photo

The corner bay of the Wister Education Center provides a moment of intimate seating within a larger space.

The small space of this Butler's Pantry uses color and lighting to create a concentrated version of the design motives found in the rest of the house.

An elegant Soane-designed stair (left) inspired the new Archer & Buchanan interpretation (center) for the stone farmhouse at Big Bend (right).

MERCER HILL FARM

Coatesville, Pennsylvania

WHEN THE VAST KING RANCH in Texas was looking for land in the northeast to fatten cattle on route to market after World War II, they bought several thousand acres in southern Chester County. Forty years later, when market conditions changed in the beef cattle business, the Brandywine Conservancy was able to acquire land from the Ranch and placed many 100-acre parcels under conservation easements. This property belonged to the Mercer family in the 1890s and is now known as Mercer Hill Farm. The site features original buildings, now re-envisioned, as well as new stables, tenant house, and a car barn.

The extant c. 1750 farmhouse (with 1800 and 1820 additions) has evolved through renovations inside to be comfortable for modern use and reflects both period detail and contemporary needs. The ruins of a massive bank barn lost to a fire in the 1950s formed the base for a new structure. A smaller bank barn was inserted within the foundation ruin, innovatively setting the upper six horse stalls on the grade of the barn bridge with access to both the upper stable yard and a center aisle. This allows for utility storage below, which opens to a lower stable yard framed by the original barn's stone walls. A surviving cattle loafing shed to the west has been transformed into a practical eleven-stall barn with a large tack room, double wash stall, and lower stable yard access as well as direct field turn-out. Both stables benefit from hay storage above to simplify feeding and share a single discrete manure pit within the antique walls.

The new car barn houses antique automobiles and serves as an entertainment pavilion for family and friends. Both the house and car barn showcase the owners' various collections of found art and artifacts. The modular tenant house was designed by Archer & Buchanan as an age-in-place residence for the senior generation.

RATHBURN HALL

Grove City College, Grove City, Pennsylvania

GROVE CITY COLLEGE is an independent Christian liberal arts college in Western Pennsylvania. The picturesque campus was planned by the Olmsted Brothers and Collegiate Gothic is the dominant building style. The 16,500-square-foot Rathburn Hall—together with the nearby 1929 gothic-style Harbison Chapel—is the center of spiritual life on campus. The facility serves as the home for the Dean of the Chapel and over 23 student-run ministries. A large fellowship hall, a great room/board room, seminar rooms, and meeting spaces allow the College to broaden institutional outreach, spiritual fellowship, and social programming. It also provides a venue for conferences and forums.

The materials and detailing of Rathburn Hall are compatible to the existing buildings on campus and the design takes advantage of the site conditions to make each façade unique. The south face forms a quiet backdrop for the chapel while the north is animated with a multi-story bay that anchors the building to the slope at the edge of the woods.

Principal in Charge: Dan Russoniello, AIA, LEED AP

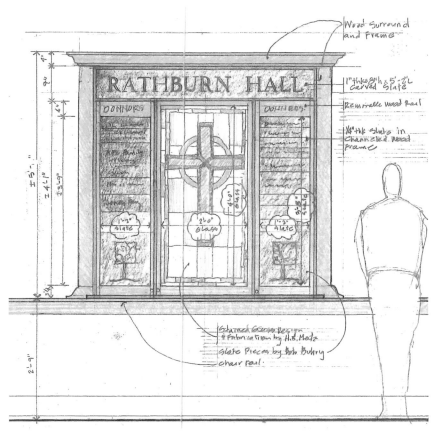

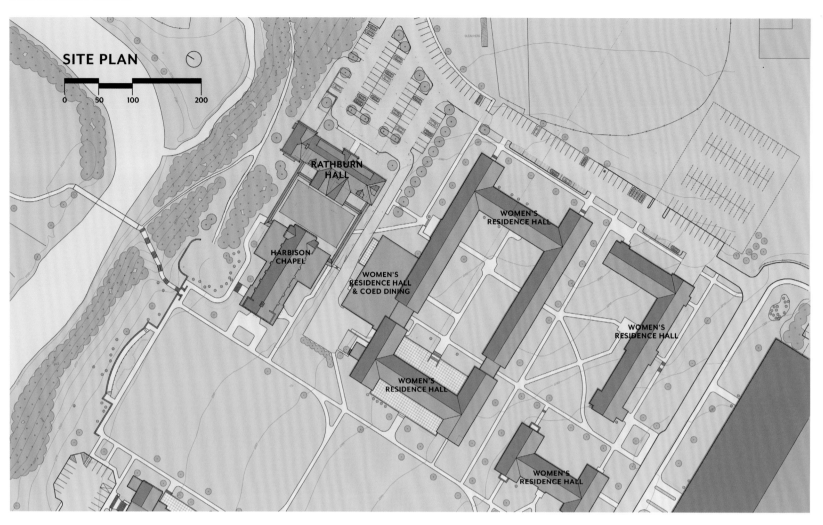

SITE PLAN

0 50 100 200

RATHBURN HALL

HARBISON CHAPEL

WOMEN'S RESIDENCE HALL & COED DINING

WOMEN'S RESIDENCE HALL

WOMEN'S RESIDENCE HALL

WOMEN'S RESIDENCE HALL

WOMEN'S RESIDENCE HALL

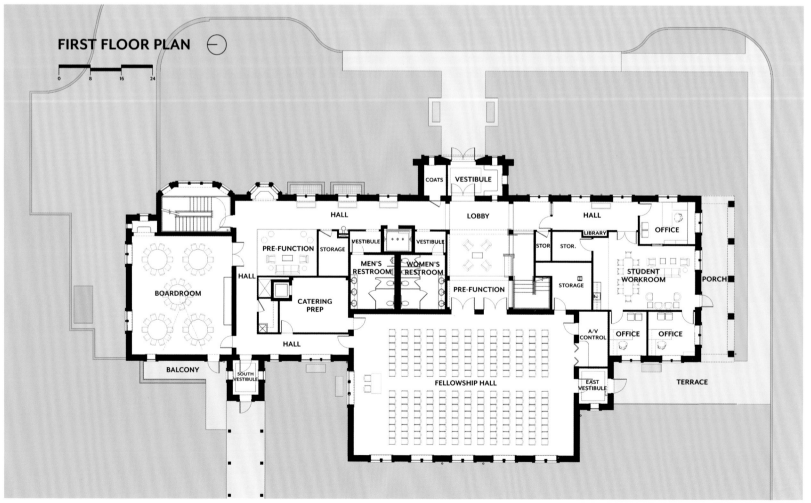

FIRST FLOOR PLAN

0 8 16 24

COATS | VESTIBULE

HALL | LOBBY | HALL

PRE-FUNCTION | STORAGE | VESTIBULE | VESTIBULE | LIBRARY | OFFICE

STOR | STOR.

BOARDROOM | HALL | MEN'S RESTROOM | WOMEN'S RESTROOM | STUDENT WORKROOM | PORCH

CATERING PREP | PRE-FUNCTION | STORAGE

HALL

A/V CONTROL | OFFICE | OFFICE

BALCONY | SOUTH VESTIBULE | EAST VESTIBULE | TERRACE

FELLOWSHIP HALL

GREENVILLE CONTEMPORARY

Chadds Ford, Pennsylvania

FOR THIS RESIDENCE, Archer & Buchanan tailored American Prairie and English Arts & Crafts aesthetics with a rational plan to make a contemporary building of extraordinary harmony and interest. Emphasis on the geometric forms and ornamental spareness result in a design that combines formality of organization with simplicity of forms. The tapered brick piers are tied together with shallow brick segmental arches that delineate each functional room within the open plan.

The primary living spaces are all on one floor split by the entrance and stair hall, which separate the kitchen and dining room from the great room and master suite. The placement on the site takes advantage of a slope to include several bedrooms, a home gym, and sewing room on a lower level where they open directly to the south lawn. The generous center stair also makes a strong connection between the upper living spaces and lower porch.

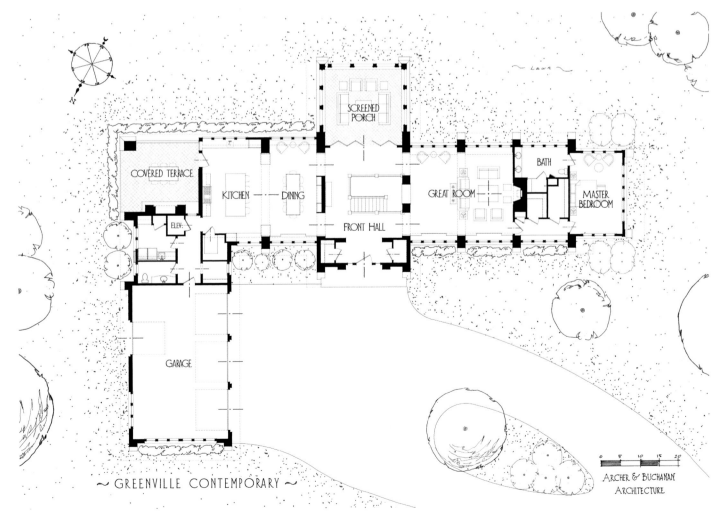

~ GREENVILLE CONTEMPORARY ~

COVERED TERRACE

KITCHEN • DINING

ELEV.

SCREENED PORCH

FRONT HALL

GREAT ROOM

BATH

MASTER BEDROOM

GARAGE

ARCHER & BUCHANAN ARCHITECTURE

LEANING TIMBER HAUS

Newtown Square, Pennsylvania

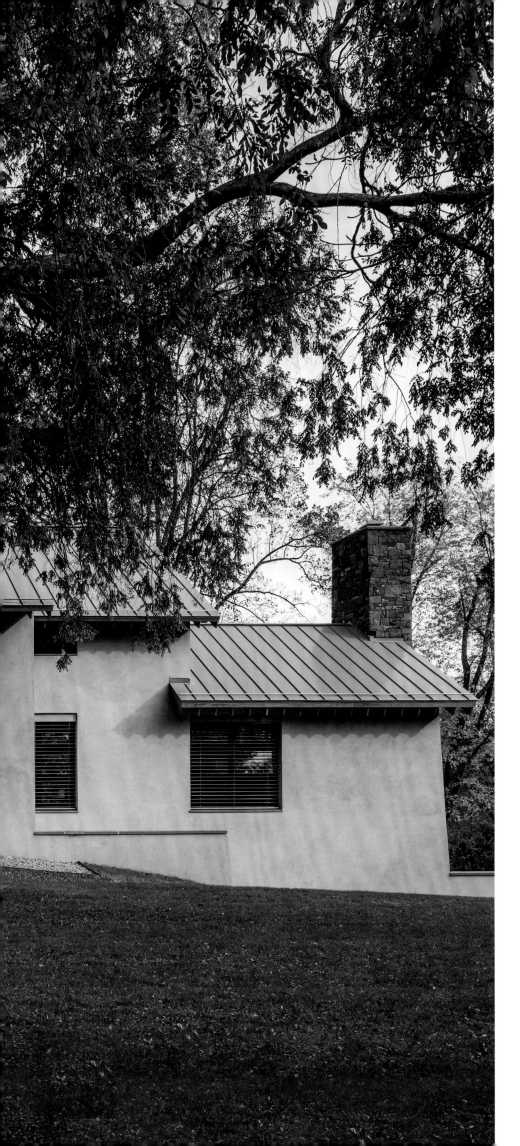

THE EXPOSED TIMBERS of this house form an elegant armature that define the indoor and outdoor living spaces. The entrance façade is marked by a two-story angled bracing and the visible interior stair enclosed like a special object in a glass case. The coplanar gabled roof and timber framing modules are the organizing features of a sophisticated play between solids and voids and glass and opaque walls. The leaning beams at both the front and back elevations enliven the ensemble.

The deceptive simplicity of the exterior extends indoors via a quiet palette of materials, colors, and details that relate to the overall structure. This inside/outside approach enables the interior to flow through the open plan to the outdoor spaces that cascade down the hillside. This project illustrates how a modest program can generate visual interest through attentive detailing.

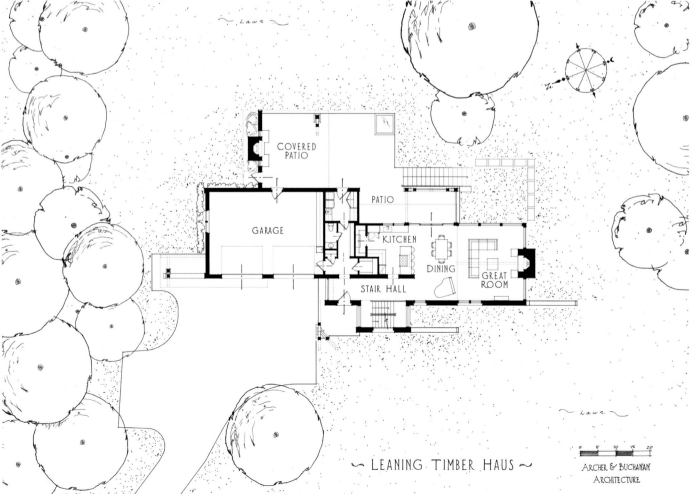

~ LEANING TIMBER HAUS ~

ARCHER & BUCHANAN
ARCHITECTURE

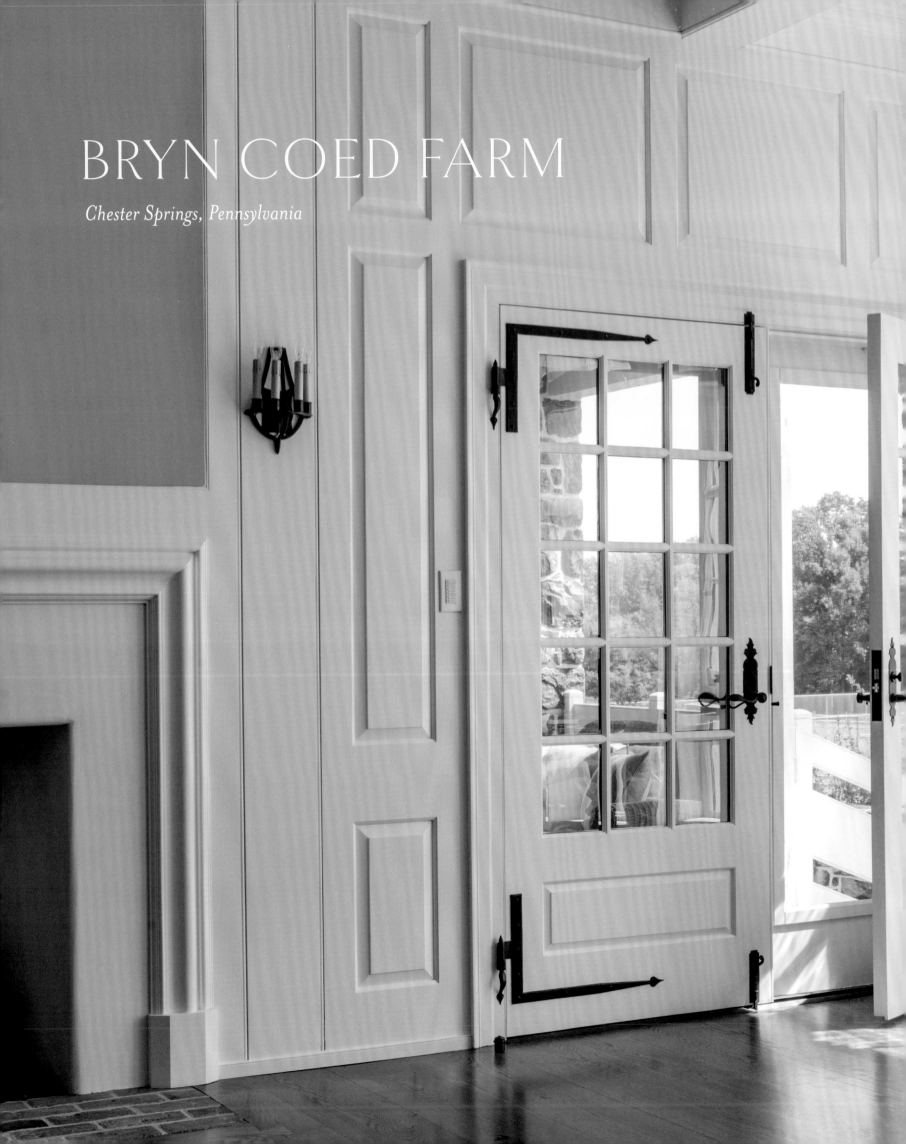

BRYN COED FARM

Chester Springs, Pennsylvania

IN 1928, R. BROGNARD OKIE began working with Supreme Court Justice Owen J. Roberts to revitalize a vast farm property in Chester County. Located below a ridge parallel to the Great Valley, the existing farmhouse had spectacular views. Roberts named the 700-acre farm "Bryn Coed," which translates to "Wooded Hill" in the native Welsh of his forebears. After Okie's renovations and expansion, Roberts' house retained the original eighteenth-century farmhouse sensibility replete with simple furnishings and an old walk-in cooking fireplace that dominated the living room. Bryn Coed became a family retreat and Justice Roberts took an active interest in the buildings and operations of the huge farm. The main house was only one aspect of the refurbished complex; from the beginning of his involvement, Okie worked with landscape architect Thomas Sears to plan the entrance drive and locations for ancillary buildings, terraces, and gardens.

For new owners, who fell in love with the property, Archer & Buchanan built upon Okie and Sears' original design to accommodate the client's large family and lifestyle. A deep, two-story addition replaces the former one-story service wing but preserves the same footprint. Subtle moves in the manner of Okie help the large, new spaces remain subordinate to the 1928 core. The single-story walls in the same brown fieldstone are a natural extension of Okie's work. On the south side, all of the original terrace walls survive and keep the definition of the main part of the house intact. The extension features stone and frame construction with a glazed arcade. Its visual weight is intentionally reduced in comparison to the older parts of the house. The plan development also respects Okie's progression of stepping the extensions and using broad areas of glass to diminish the mass perceived from the outside and to brighten rooms within.

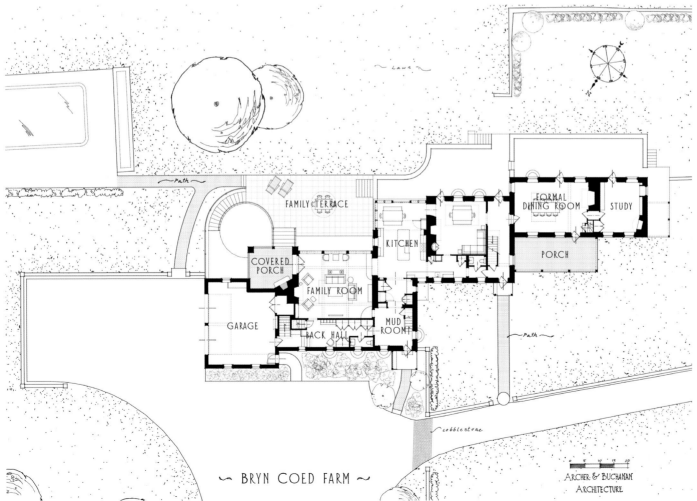

~ BRYN COED FARM ~

ARCHER & BUCHANAN
ARCHITECTURE

HOME BRED FARM

Gladwyne, Pennsylvania

THE DESIGN FOR HOME BRED FARM plays with the concept of a rustic home and barn becoming co-joined as a singular residence. Sited on a 11.5-acre parcel on Philadelphia's Main Line, the architecture of the exterior is a blend of invention and regional tradition. The main entrance is denoted by a pergola adjacent to the barn form, which is marked by a monumental arched window and pediment. The barn shape remains dominant at the rear elevation but is rendered differently with an array of smaller windows. A large wrap-around porch at the back of the house provides both visual and physical links between the indoors and outdoors. The interior features an expansive, timber-framed Great Room specifically designed for entertaining. Rough-sawn Douglas fir timbers and reclaimed wood flooring add a natural warmth while other details, such as the custom hardware, bring a small-scale tactile quality to this large space.

Although it defies a defined architectural style, this new residence unites its Main Line antecedents with clearly communicated parts of a contemporary program.

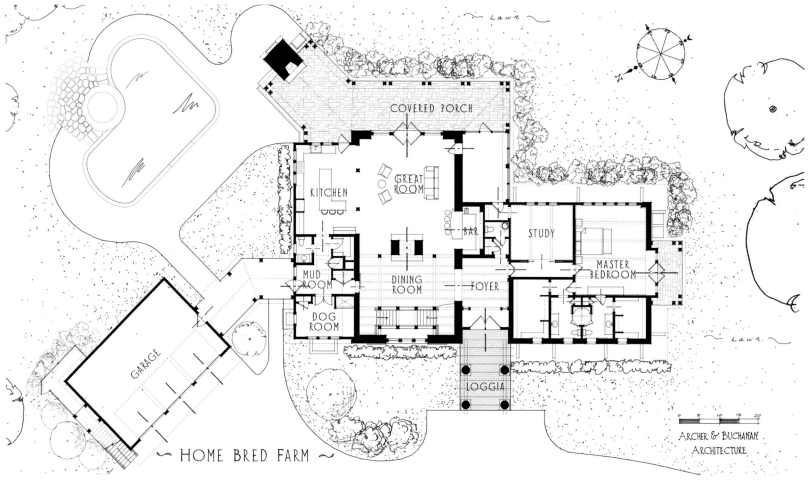

COVERED PORCH

KITCHEN

GREAT ROOM

BAR

STUDY

MASTER BEDROOM

MUD ROOM

DINING ROOM

FOYER

DOG ROOM

GARAGE

LOGGIA

~ HOME BRED FARM ~

ARCHER & BUCHANAN ARCHITECTURE

MATERIALS
& DETAILS

CUSTOM DESIGN AND CRAFT in construction persists across all stylistic expressions, traditional to contemporary. Fluency is fully illustrated within Archer & Buchanan's portfolio with materials and details supporting the design and concepts of every project. Architect Louis Kahn famously captured the symbiotic relationship between materials and details when he asked, "What does a brick want to be?" But even as architects of the Modern Movement emphasized and celebrated innate qualities of materials, such as form lines in concrete or connection details in steel, architects of traditional architecture retained a time-honored attitude. Regional availability of raw materials and craftsmen working closely with designers has always been an integral part of the design process. Functionality and honesty of expression in architecture is not new, it is the universal language of design made manifest.

Different types of masonry offer various opportunities for details, such as the stylized millstone in the rubble masonry (top) and the ornamental patterns in the brick (below).

A large part of the artistry in timber framing is the joinery in traditional pegged mortise and tenon connections.

Ever since architecture became a profession distinct from the construction trades and master builders, the role of the designer has been to create a legible description of the intended work through drawings, models, and written instructions. In much of the construction that occurs today, the architect's role stops before, or rapidly diminishes during the actual building. The best completed projects, at any size or style, are always the result of a continual partnership between design and construction. Archer & Buchanan is firmly in the position of seeing projects through from conception to occupancy. The successful journey from idea to finished building relies on a steady relationship.

When looking closely at the materials incorporated in the firm's projects there is a sense that the design details and execution are in concert. The materials used give each architectural statement continuity and clarity. Details are like punctuation or grammar within a written page; they guide, inform, and complete the big picture. The iconic rubble stone construction for a new barn in southern Chester County, for instance, is derived from eighteenth-century bank barn precedents. This element upholds the design vision for this particular farm compound and is appropriate to the historic landscape. The outcome is dependent on the skill of the mason, but preliminary review of stone samples by the architect are necessary for determining how colors and sizes of stone are mixed and how the joints are treated, and in this case, how the millstone is incorporated.

Use of brick, like almost any other material, can be utilitarian or make a statement. Either way, the outcome underscores the design and the finesse of the installer. In the case of a construction office on the Main Line, the exterior features brick of different colors, bonding, and shapes to demonstrate the quality and care the construction company brings to its projects. Archer & Buchanan's design effects are more subtle in the Greenville Contemporary house illustrated at the beginning of this essay (p. 178). Tapered piers and large segmental arches are exceptionally executed using unusual brick shapes and masonry expertise to create perfect alignment and coursing.

For the firm's residential work, wood remains a primary structural, cladding, and finish material. Structural timber joinery is an art form with a long history virtually unlimited in its methods. There is craft in joinery with pegged connections, but steel fasteners and supplemental pieces like tension rods can be elegant in a different way. The timber framing at the contemporary Mill Creek House has a completely divergent appeal than the traditional barn at Springbrook Farm, which serves as a teaching facility for children with disabilities. Yet another example, the Lenfest Center, employs a mix of timber and metal components.

Archer & Buchanan's appreciation of the inventiveness of the late-nineteenth-century shingle style has given rise to new interpretations using wood as a versatile exterior material. From roof and wall shingles to clapboard and board and batten siding, the firm utilizes a wood membrane to create a variety of geometrical shapes and as a neutral backdrop for more elaborate door and window openings and spacious porches. Wooden moldings provide the definition for openings, material transitions, and cornices. For a residence in Chestnut Hill, not far from downtown Philadelphia, Archer & Buchanan contrasts the visual lightness of the shingling to heavier wood elements and stone masonry.

Interior woodwork is a design specialty successfully achieved by the ability to think in three dimensions and resolve geometries in documentation before materials are purchased and the installation begins. Whether painted, built-up moldings or flat trims with natural finishes, elements must be appropriately sized for their spaces and have logical starting and stopping places. Schemes can begin simply and intensify to moments that mark points of interest. Sophisticated millwork is not just about complexity and using different profiles. The early-twentieth-century architect, R. Brognard Okie, was a master of subtlety in the way he used low profiles and simple beaded edges to create geometrical wall patterns. Similarly, the Art & Crafts movement stressed fine materials and simple exposed joinery to make strong design statements. Archer & Buchanan likewise utilizes a range of interior woodwork to complement its designs.

The new addition at Mill Creek recreates the framing of the existing residence as an open porch boldly defined in vivid colors.

Slate, mica schist, and wood shingling create a sensual composition.

The sweep of the staircase to a curved overlook complements the round knuckle in the building plan.

Ornamental ironwork and wood joinery combine to create an abstract composition of forms.

Ironwork allows for many whimsical touches.

The wood and metal each express their character in these post bases in the Asian–Inspired Residence.

Included in the realm of interior woodwork, staircases hold pride of place. The just-right balance of form and detail, whether a straight run or sweeping curve, challenges the architect's imagination and the builder's expertise. Stairs are also an opportunity to utilize different materials and trades together to enrich the interior environment.

In addition to the "sticks and bricks" that give a project character, use of other materials such as glass, metals, and special finishes can create unique moments. Such moments can include the insertion of a found object such as the shell niche repurposed in a powder room at Mercer Hill. Antique lock boxes or tin candle holders reimagined as electric lights were favorites of Brognard Okie and remain effective accents today. Colored glass or specialty hardware can impart beauty or some whimsy into a project, such as at Starry Night Farm. Even as materials have certain inherent qualities that fine design and craftsmanship can accentuate, details and detailing are a different, but related art. Belying complexity, Archer & Buchanan's Asian-Inspired Residence adapts traditional Asian design to create exquisite details for wall screens, woodwork, and metal post bases for a comfortable minimalism.

Artistry and imagination are like connective tissue in the work of Archer & Buchanan. Designs may be inspired by local, regional, and international precedents; certainly, great examples from the past come into play. Underscoring and completing each vision are the individual elements and the selected materials that make a project rich and whole. The firm's commitment to considered design options and a collaborative way of working with clients, craftsmen, and constructors is a hallmark. Opportunities that tap Archer & Buchanan's breadth of experience also gives rise to invention as evidenced by the projects in this book.

Photography by: Don Pearse Photographers, Jim Graham Photography, Tom Crane Photography, Leslie W. Kipp, Angle Eye Photography, Archer & Buchanan Architecture, Jana Bannan Photography

SPEAKMAN HILL FARM

Unionville, Pennsylvania

THE SPEAKMAN HILL FARM is entirely new construction that evokes specific precedents in southern Chester County architecture. The brick residential design of the eighteenth and early-nineteenth centuries has characteristic pent eaves and coved cornices that reappear in this project. The south gable end of the house calls out the year completed in darker "clinker" bricks, a local tradition. The adjacent bank barn appears to be a fresh restoration with its salvaged stone end gable with crown pointing and forebay on tapered piers.

There is more to this new narrative as is evidenced in the rear elevation. There is an extra story due to the sloping site and it features a full-height semicircular bay with curved sash windows. The gesture, including the accompanying rear terrace with its curved steps and garden walls, suggest a later, nineteenth-century expansion into the landscape.

CANARY COTTAGE

Wayne, Pennsylvania

BEHIND THE FORMAL FAÇADE of the Canary Cottage is an open plan optimized for family living. Completely at home in its Main Line setting, this house invites easy movement through rooms to the rear where windows and porches animate the composition. Creating a sequence of experiences is a salient feature in the work of Archer & Buchanan. That it happens so seamlessly is a testament to how well the firm integrates traditional architecture as a point of departure rather than a set of rules to be explicitly followed.

The deceptively basic entrance leads to a sophisticated plan and its three-dimensional realization of the entire house. There is a wonderful flow between the various zones of the formal front entrance, living/ dining room, and the generous informal family space. Together, these rooms comprise about half of the first-floor footprint. Not only does each zone have a different character inside, they also have different relationships to adjacent covered and open outdoor areas. The refined details throughout hold everything together and reward the eye.

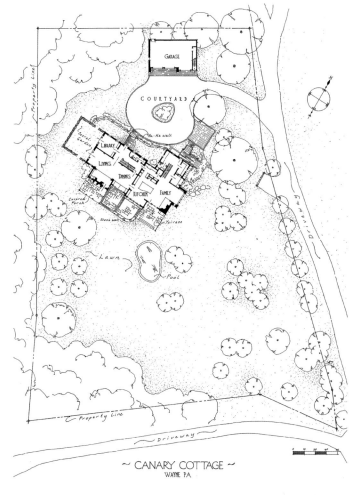

~ CANARY COTTAGE ~
WAYNE, P.A.

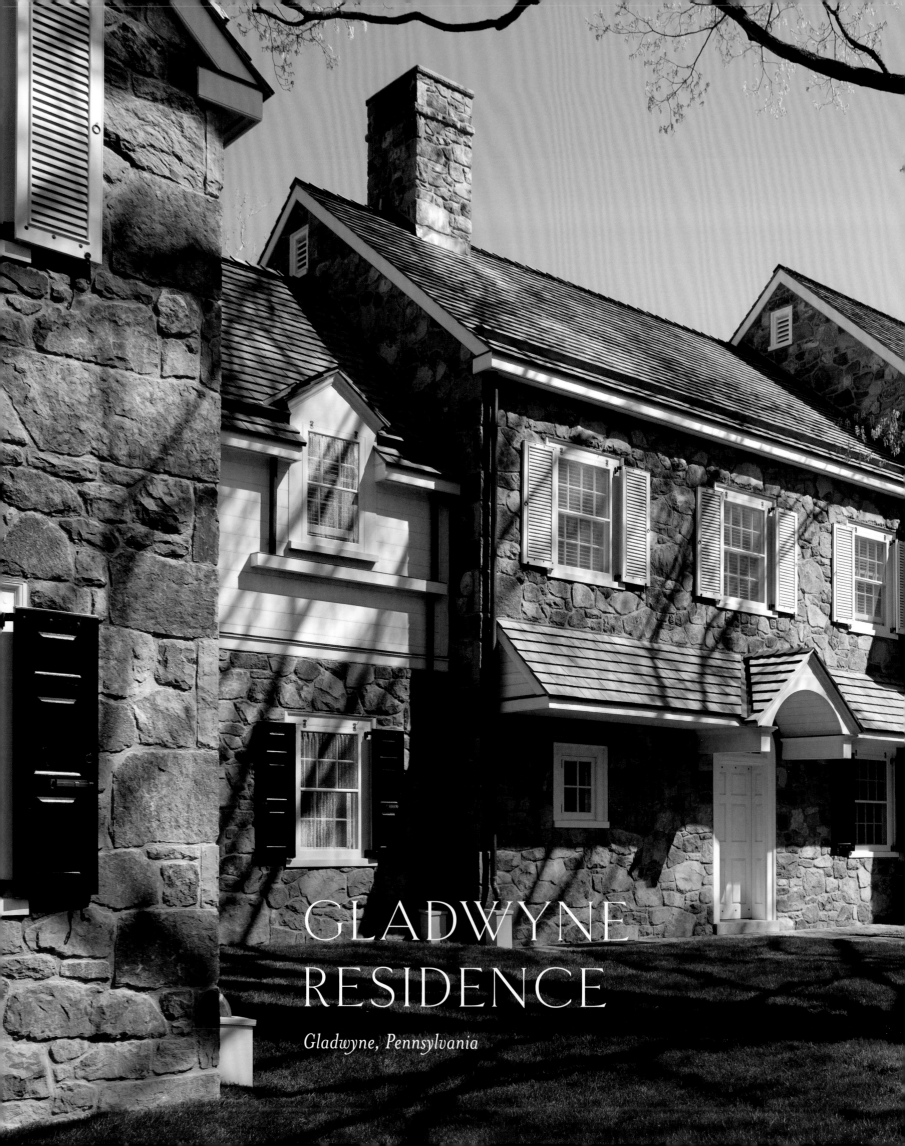

GLADWYNE RESIDENCE

Gladwyne, Pennsylvania

THIS NEW RESIDENCE in Gladwyne reinterprets traditional farmhouse design in the manner of architect R. Brognard Okie. Like many of Okie's projects, the design for this 7,800-square-foot house demanded an imaginative way of accommodating all of the program into traditional forms typically found in smaller buildings. Archer & Buchanan's solution was to have the architecture create a story based on successive additions, but with a coherence that is rare in older prototypes. The geometrical forms are based on specific responses to the internal program while being artfully composed for exterior effect.

The house is sited to preserve mature trees and create multi-level terraces at the rear. The setting heightens the sense of age and inevitability of the building. Inside, the plan separates the traditional formal spaces from family areas using a front to back stair hall as a delineator. In a similar vein, the interior details become less elaborate in the less-formal living areas. The design of this new house is imbued with spirit of Okie and advances his influence into a new century.

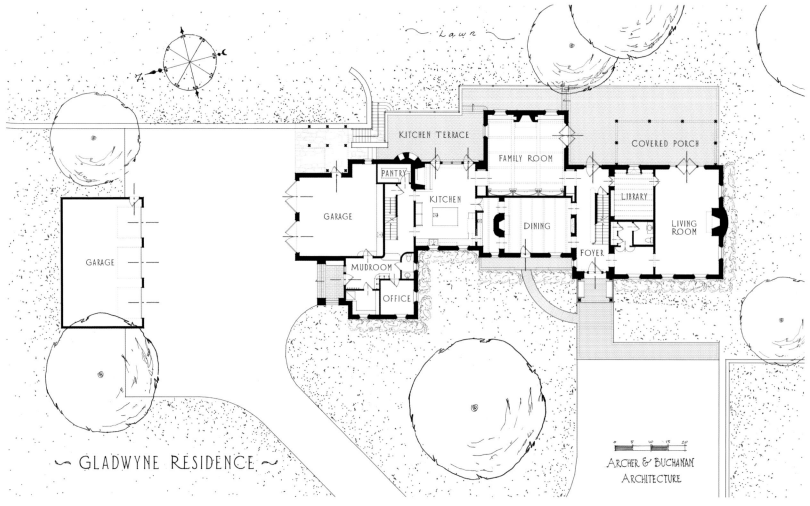

~ GLADWYNE RESIDENCE ~

ARCHER & BUCHANAN
ARCHITECTURE

1898 STABLE RESIDENCE

Wayne, Pennsylvania

CARRIAGE HOUSES AND STABLES were vital components of turn-of-the-century country and suburban estates. Often, they mimicked the main house with similar design themes and details. This large carriage house was designed in the Jacobean style by William Price as part of a grand estate. The carriage house was eventually converted into an independent residence but underwent few alterations since the parcel was initially divided.

The original building had horse stalls, space for carriages, and living quarters for the staff who were responsible for the horses and buggies and later, for automobiles. To provide all of the modern family amenities in a distinctive late-nineteenth-century structure, the project entailed extensive restoration. Changes included new garage doors compatible to extant masonry openings as well as subtle modifications to other door and window openings. On the interior, some of the decorative features were retained such as the fireplaces and exposed heavy timber. The overall effect maintains the heritage of Price's design while clearly supporting a contemporary residential use.

SOUTH ELEVATION

ALL AROUND FARM

Gwynedd Valley, Pennsylvania

THIS FORMERLY DECREPIT late-nineteenth-century carriage and show barn at All Around Farm has been imaginatively transformed. Now a robust four-bedroom residence, the building retains some of the stabling functions in a beautifully integrated result. Over the years, the 9,750-square-foot structure was used for car storage and later it became Junie Kulp, Jr.'s internationally recognized show barn. Essentially neglected otherwise, the stone and timber-framed barn remained structurally sound and captured the imagination of the new owners and Archer & Buchanan.

The very large volume of the original central block carriage barn with its magnificent timber framing logically suggested an open plan for the kitchen, living, and dining rooms with the bedrooms accommodated in the spacious loft above. The projecting wings that form two sides of the entry court retain the stable uses, converting only one portion into a garage bay. The dark color scheme for the new woodwork complement the original exposed structure for a warm, inviting core space. The lofts above are airy in contrast and take advantage of the generous volumes enabled by the gambrel roof.

The adaptive reuse of this particular barn illustrates an ideal confluence of Archer & Buchanan's facility with equestrian facilities, knowledge of historical settings, and a sensitivity for blending the old and the new.

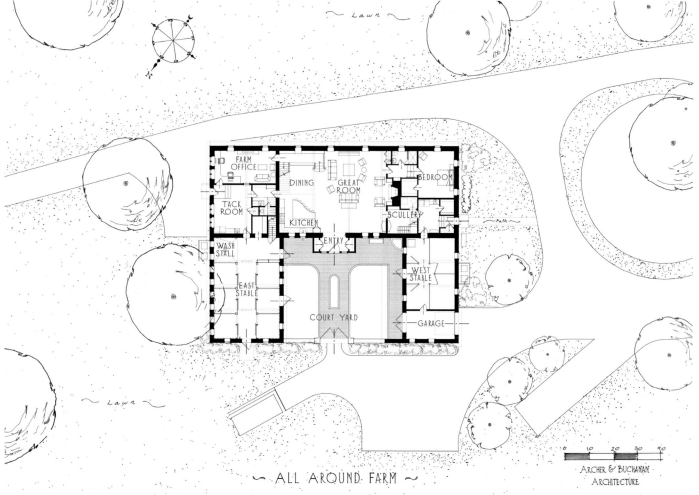

~ ALL AROUND FARM ~

ARCHER & BUCHANAN
ARCHITECTURE

ARCHIVE

Selected Work from 1996–2021

CONNORS RESIDENCE | 1996

New Residence

Radnor, PA

JUPITER ISLAND RESIDENCE | 1996

New Residence

Jupiter, FL

DELANCEY ST RENOVATION | 1997

Addition/Alteration

Philadelphia, PA

NEWTOWN SQ RESIDENCE | 1997

Addition/Alteration

Radnor, PA

ROCKING HORSE FARM | 1997

New Construction

Newlin, PA

ROSS LIBRARY ADDITION | 1997

Addition/Alteration

Bryn Mawr, PA

BEAVER DAM RESIDENCE | 1998

New Residence

Unionville, PA

CHARLES ALLEN RESIDENCE | 1998

Addition/Alteration

Gladwyne, PA

MARSHALL SQUARE PARK | 1998

Five New Residences

West Chester, PA

RITTENHOUSE APARTMENT | 1998

Addition/Alteration

Philadelphia, PA

SCHOLL RESIDENCE | 1998

New Residence

West Chester, PA

TUNBRIDGE ROAD | 1998

New Residence

Bryn Mawr, PA

MONTCHANIN | 1999

New Residence

Montchanin, DE

CHESAPEAKE BAY FARM | 1999

New Residence

Budds Landing, MD

MERCER HILL COTTAGE | 1999

New Construction

Coatesville, PA

MILL CREEK RESIDENCE | 1999

Addition/Alteration

Gladwyne, PA

"OUT OF AFRICA" | 1999

New Residence

Chester Springs, PA

ROSEDON CARRIAGE HOUSE | 1999

New Construction

Devon, PA

SPUR OF THE MOMENT FARM | 1999

New Construction

Unionville, PA

WELCOME HERE FARM | 1999

New Construction

Chatham, PA

76 FARM | 2000

Addition/Alteration

Berwyn, PA

CANNON HILL | 2000

New Construction

Chadds Ford, PA

LEOPARD LAKE RESIDENCE | 2000

New Residence

Berwyn, PA

MATLACK HOUSE | 2000

Addition/Alteration

Wayne, PA

ARDROSSAN RESIDENCE | 2001

New Residence

Wayne, PA

BRIGHT RESIDENCE | 2001

Addition/Alteration

Unionville, PA

CHARLES STOKES RESIDENCE | 2001

Addition/Alteration

Narberth, PA

BANK BARN STUDIO | 2001

New Construction

Berwyn, PA

HOUYHNHNM FARM | 2001

New Residence

Unionville, PA

RONALD MCDONALD HOUSE | 2001

Institutional

Philadelphia, PA

ROSS COMMONS | 2001

Institutional

Philadelphia, PA

THAYER RESIDENCE | 2001

Addition/Alteration

Devon, PA

WEST VIEW FARM ARENA | 2001

Equestrian

Newlin, PA

BRIGADOON | 2002

New Construction

Devon, PA

BRIGHT HOLLOW FARM | 2002

New Construction

West Grove, PA

CENTERVILLE RESIDENCE | 2002

Addition/Alteration

Wilmington, DE

MAPLE HILL BARN | 2002

Addition/Alteration

Gladwyne, PA

ROSEDON | 2002

Addition/Alteration

Devon, PA

STRAWBRIDGE COURT | 2002

New Construction

Wynnewood, PA

TEMPLIN ROAD RESIDENCE | 2002

New Residence

Glenmoore, PA

WILLISTOWN RESIDENCE | 2002

New Residence

Willistown, PA

BOHEMIA MANOR FARM | 2003

Addition/Alteration

Chesapeake City, MD

GARDEN LANE ADDITIONS | 2003

Addition/Alteration

Bryn Mawr, PA

HAVERFORD ADDITION | 2003

Addition/Alteration

Haverford, PA

N. ROSE LANE RESIDENCE | 2003

Addition/Alteration

Bryn Mawr, PA

STARRY NIGHT FARM | 2003

New Construction

Unionville, PA

STONE LEA FARM | 2003

Addition/Alteration

Conowingo, MD

WALTER DURHAM HOUSE | 2003

Addition/Alteration

Gladwyne, PA

YOUNGSFORD RD RESIDENCE | 2003

New Residence

Gladwyne, PA

BRYN MAWR RENOVATION | 2004

Addition/Alteration

Bryn Mawr, PA

FT WASHINGTON RESIDENCE | 2004

New Residence

Fort Washington, PA

GREAT SPRINGS RESIDENCE | 2004

New Residence

Bryn Mawr, PA

ROCKLAND ROAD ADDITION | 2004

Addition/Alteration

Montchanin, DE

SPRING BROOK FARM | 2004

New Construction

Pocopson, PA

SPRINGDELL RESIDENCE | 2004

New Residence

Springdell, PA

THE WHIP TAVERN | 2004

Commercial

Chatham, PA

TWO SISTERS FARM | 2004

Equestrian

East Fallowfield, PA

WAY ROAD RESIDENCE | 2004

New Residence

Centerville, PA

BLUEDOG FARM BARN | 2005

New Construction

Willistown, PA

DRAPER WALSH STADIUM | 2005

Institutional

Immaculata University, Immaculata, PA

FOURTH HOLE FARM | 2005

Addition/Alteration

Chestnut Hill, PA

NATURE PAVILION | 2005

Folly

Glenmoore, PA

ROOSEVELT LIBRARY WING | 2005

Addition/Alteration

Coatesville, PA

ABENDRUH | 2006

Addition/Alteration

Gwynedd, PA

AMELIA S. GIVIN LIBRARY | 2006

Addition/Alteration

Mt. Holly Springs, PA

BROOK ROAD RESIDENCE | 2006

Addition/Alteration

St. Davids, PA

DERRY BAWN | 2006

New Residence

Willistown, PA

BRIGADOON CONSERVATORY | 2006

Addition/Alteration

Devon, PA

MERION POOLHOUSE | 2006

New Construction

Merion Station, PA

MINE ROAD FARM | 2006

Addition/Alteration

Malvern, PA

OLD GULPH RD RESIDENCE | 2006

Addition/Alteration

Villanova, PA

SPA ADDITION | 2006

New Construction

Ardmore, PA

TEA HOUSE | 2006

Folly

Chestnut Hill, PA

BROOK FARM | 2007

New Construction

Wayne, PA

CHESHIRE HUNT STABLE | 2007

Equestrian

Unionville, PA

EL BRIO RANCH | 2007

Addition/Alteration

East Fallowfield, PA

HAMILTON ST RESIDENCE | 2007

Addition/Alteration

Philadelphia, PA

PETRILLO RESIDENCE | 2007

New Residence

Kennett Square, PA

OXFORD RESIDENCE | 2007

New Residence

Oxford, PA

ROSEMONT COTTAGE | 2007

Addition/Alteration

Rosemont, PA

STUBENBERG ARENA | 2007

Equestrian

West Grove, PA

SUTTON TERRACE | 2007

Commercial

Bala Cynwyd, PA

ANDERSON PLACE | 2008

Addition/Alteration

Phoenixville, PA

ADMISSIONS OFFICE | 2008

Institutional

Swarthmore College, Swarthmore, PA

AU SOLIEL D'OR | 2008

Barn Reconstruction

Malvern, PA

CHESTNUT HILL RESIDENCE | 2008

New Residence

Chestnut Hill, PA

DODGER RUN FARM | 2008

New Construction

Unionville, PA

GUEST HOUSE & GARAGE | 2008

Addition/Alteration

Berwyn, PA

WILMINGTON RESIDENCE | 2008

Addition/Alteration

Wilmington, DE

BBC TAVERN | 2009

Commercial

Greenville, DE

BLUE BELL RESIDENCE | 2009

Addition/Alteration

Blue Bell, PA

E B MAHONEY OFFICE | 2009

Commercial

Bryn Mawr, PA

FAIRLAWN | 2009

Addition/Alteration

Devon, PA

KIMBERTON BARN | 2009

Addition/Alteration

Kimberton, PA

KNOTT RESIDENCE | 2009

Addition/Alteration

Monkton, MD

STONE RIDGE RESIDENCE | 2009

New Residence

Villanova, PA

SUTTON RESIDENCE | 2009

New Residence

Avalon, NJ

WEISSENBERGER RESIDENCE | 2009

New Residence

Villanova, PA

CRUM CREEK FARM | 2010

Addition/Alteration

Berwyn, PA

PAPER MILL HOUSE | 2010

Addition/Alteration

Newtown Square, PA

PETTIT RESIDENCE | 2010

Addition/Alteration

Radnor, PA

PRESIDENT'S OFFICE | 2010

Institutional

Swarthmore College, Swarthmore, PA

ROCKFORD PARK HOUSE | 2010

New Residence

Wilmington, MD

ROCKY HILL BARN | 2010

Equestrian

Chadds Ford, PA

SUNROOM | 2010

Addition/Alteration

Bryn Mawr, PA

THORNBURY ADDITION | 2010

Addition/Alteration

Thornbury, PA

WEATHERFIELD POOL HOUSE | 2010

New Construction

Newtown, PA

FOX HOLLOW | 2011

New Residence

Chadds Ford, PA

NORTH CHURCH RESIDENCE | 2011

Addition/Alteration

West Chester, PA

PORTER TROPHY ROOM | 2011

Addition/Alteration

Chadds Ford, PA

TRIMBLE'S FORD DANCE BARN | 2011

Folly

West Chester, PA

TRUE PROSPECT FARM | 2011

New Residence

West Grove, PA

CHURCH OF THE HOLY TRINITY | 2012

Institutional

West Chester, PA

FAIRVILLE RESIDENCE | 2012

New Residence

Chadds Ford, PA

ROWLAND RD BEACH HOUSES | 2012

New Residences

Fairfield, CT

TIMBERFRAME PAVILION | 2012

Folly

Gladwyne, PA

TUNNEL FARM | 2012

Addition/Alteration

Ambler, PA

BRYN MAWR DEVELOPMENT | 2013

Commercial

Bryn Mawr, PA

GREENBRIAR RESIDENCE | 2013

Addition/Alteration

Paoli, PA

KOSHER COMMISSARY | 2013

Commercial

King of Prussia, PA

MALVERN RESIDENCE | 2013

New Residence

Malvern, PA

PORTER CONST. OFFICE | 2013

Institutional

Chadds Ford, PA

RED CLAY FARM | 2013

Addition/Alteration

Kennett Square, PA

SHEAFF LANE | 2013

Addition/Alteration

Ft. Washington, PA

TWINBROOK TUDOR | 2013

Addition/Alteration

Berwyn, PA

BRYN MAWR RESIDENCE | 2013

Addition/Alteration

Bryn Mawr, PA

CENTER FOR AUTISM | 2014

Institutional

Philadelphia, PA

DEEPOP PARTY BARN | 2014

Folly

Berwyn, PA

GREEN LANE COTTAGE | 2014

New Residence

Malvern, PA

LANTERN LANE | 2014

New Residence

Blue Bell, PA

MONTCHANIN RD RESIDENCE | 2014

New Residence

Wilmington, DE

PEQUEA RESIDENCE | 2014

New Residence

Pequea Township, PA

ROSE LANE RESIDENCE | 2014

Addition/Alteration

Haverford, PA

SPORTS COURT PAVILION | 2014

Folly

Penn Valley, PA

SUNNY HIGH | 2014

Addition/Alteration

Wayne, PA

CANNERY BARN | 2015

Equestrian

Coatesville, PA

COLBY'S RUN | 2015

New Residence

Villanova, PA

GWYNEDD HOUSE | 2015

New Residence

Lower Gwynedd, PA

DEVON HORSE SHOW PAVILION | 2015

Institutional

Devon, PA

HARPER RESIDENCE | 2015

New Residence

Coatesville, PA

MEADOW LANE | 2015

New Residence

Berwyn, PA

ST JOSEPH'S PARISH OFFICE | 2015

Institutional

Downingtown, PA

PAINTER BARN | 2015

Institutional

Tyler Arboretum, Media, PA

TURTLE HATCH FARM | 2015

New Residence

Mechanicsburg, PA

ALPACA RUN FARM | 2016

New Residence

West Chester, PA

CHADDS FORD COTTAGE | 2016

New Residence

Chadds Ford, PA

GLEN MILLS RESIDENCE | 2016

Addition/Alteration

Glen Mills, PA

GREYSTONE BARN | 2016

Addition/Alteration

West Chester, PA

MAPLESHADE | 2016

New Residence

Malvern, PA

STABLE INTO FILM OFFICE | 2017

Addition/Alteration

Willistown, PA

HIGH STREET RESIDENCE | 2017

Addition/Alteration

West Chester, PA

HOBBIT COTTAGE | 2017

New Residence

Mosier, OR

LEESIDE FARM | 2017

Addition/Alteration

New Hope, PA

TOWERFIELD | 2017

New Residence

Villanova, PA

WILLOWDALE GRAY BARN | 2017

Commercial

Unionville, PA

HAVENWOOD | 2018

New Residence

Plumstead, PA

ST PATRICK CHURCH | 2018

Institutional

Kennett Square, PA

WORK TO RIDE | 2018

Institutional

Philadelphia, PA

HEXTON | 2019

Addition/Alteration

Fredericktown, MD

SMITHBRIDGE RD RESIDENCE | 2019

Addition/Alteration

Chadds Ford, PA

THE WILLOWS | 2019

Institutional

Radnor, PA

ARDROSSAN ESTATE | 2020

New Residence

Villanova, PA

KNOW HOWE FARM | 2020

New Construction

Cochranville, PA

MONTCHANIN RESIDENCE | 2020

Addition/Alteration

Montchanin, DE

SPORTS CAR GARAGE | 2020

New Construction

Gladwyne, PA

BIG BEND | 2021

Addition/Alteration

Chadds Ford, PA

CANNERY RESIDENCE | 2021

Addition/Alteration

Coatesville, PA

CAUFFIEL EVENT BARN | 2021

Commercial

Wilmington, DE

FERNBANK FARM WINE CELLAR | 2021

Addition/Alteration

West Chester, PA

BURIAL VAULTS | 2021

Institutional

West Laurel Hill Cemetery, Philadelphia, PA

HEADMASTER'S RECEPTION | 2021

Addition/Alteration

The Hill School, Pottstown, PA

JOSEPH PEW RESIDENCE | 2021

Addition/Alteration

Gladwyne, PA

OUR LADY OF KNOCK GROTTO | 2021

Institutional

Miraculous Medal Shrine, Philadelphia, PA

WALTON RESIDENCE | 2021

New Residence

Berwyn, PA

WENDELL DORMITORY | 2021

Addition/Alteration

The Hill School, Pottstown, PA

WINDURRA USA INDOOR ARENA | 2021

Equestrian

Cochranville, PA

ST PATRICK CHURCH LINK

Institutional | In Design

Kennett Square, PA

RAVENWOOD ORANGERIE

New Construction | In Design

Berwyn, PA

CRUM CREEK RESIDENCE

New Residence | In Design

Willistown, PA

MILL CREEK

New Residence | In Design

Gladwyne, PA

PEACHFIELD BARN

Institutional | In Design

Burlington County, NJ

EVENT BARN

Commercial | In Design

Southeastern PA

EVENT BARN

Commercial | In Design

Newtown Square, PA

BOUGH HAUS

New Residence | In Design

West Chester, PA

CHATEAU DU GATTO

New Residence | In Design

Lakeville, PA

LEWES BAY HOUSE

New Residence | In Design

Lewes, DE

THOMPSON RESIDENCE

New Residence | In Design

St. Michael's, MD

SNOW HILL RESIDENCE

Addition/Alteration | In Design

Mendham, NJ

COLLEAGUES

Alumni to Present

Suzanne Amrich
Peter Archer
Mark Avellino
Bernard Beegle
Scott Beegle
Jason Birl
Donald Bockoven
Steven Bolinger
Daniel Bryer
Richard Buchanan
Wesley Byrne
Andrew Cacchio
Tracy Carlson
Connerie Cepeda
Chris Cleary
Lucas Craig
Matthew Cramer
Travis Crum
Alex Cutrona
Bryan Cvitanov
Anna Daddario
Gina Dianna
Anthony DiValerio
Jeffrey Dolan
Andrew Donaldson-Evans
Thomas Dougherty
Alice Dowd
Danielle DuCoeur
Donald Dunham
Andrew Filipe
Jessica Fogle
C. Matthew Forsythe II
Sondra Gawlikowski
Norman Goddard

Jamie Greenland
Daniel Heron
Julie Hoffman
Christine Hofnagel
Justin Hughes
Jana Hungarter
Laura Izzo
Rebecca Jee
Robert Jiminez
Kimberly Kelley
Samuel Kim
Bradley Kline
Paul Knepley
Clark LaMotte
Amy Larchuk
Amelia Linde
Joseph Mackin, Jr.
Anne Madron
Rahul Malla
Douglas Mancuso
Diana Mann
Heather Martin
Amanda Mazie
David Mazzocco
Patrick McGrail-Peasley
Kristin McKenica
Brian McVeigh
Allison Michels
F. Patrick Mohan
Amanda Morris
Benjamin Nia
Alyssa Novak
Bridget O'Brien
Justin Olear

Christopher Olstein
Sarah Owens
Jackie Patterson
Chad Peterson
Shannon Pitt
Sonia Pluta
Joshua Pontell
Cheri Privor
Ali Pugliese
Kyle Ramey
Daniel Rau
Mary Rayner
Alexander Rice
Jennifer Roman
Daniel G. Russoniello
Daniel H. Russoniello
Scott Sampson
Antonio Scanga
John Shea
Jeffery Skourtis
Joanna Skros
Derek Stoner
Michael Stonikinis
Lily Summers
Robert Sutton
Michele Thackrah
David Thebus
Alexandria Turchi
Michael Walsh
Erinn Wenrich
Bryan Wilson
Karen Wood
Dawn Wright
Cristina Wuenschel

ACKNOWLEDGMENTS

When Peter and I opened the doors of our office in 1996 we were already "standing on the shoulders of giants," to quote Sir Isaac Newton. From the beginning, we were indebted to mentors, colleagues, building professionals, and clients who taught, encouraged, and supported our particular architectural emphasis. We are deeply grateful to practice the alchemy of traditional design motifs in the service of contemporary needs through high quality construction. Now, after twenty-five years, we have hundreds of people to thank for our good fortune.

At this stage we pause to reflect with gratitude upon all those who have been integral to the firm's growth and success. We must begin with our four parents, none with us any longer and very much missed. Next, we recognize Michele Thackrah, AIA, who began with us as an intern at Solutions Architects and has since grown within Archer & Buchanan Architecture as a staff architect, principal, and partner. The three of us would not have gotten far without our spouses, the talented artist Maria Archer; Cindy Buchanan, VMD; and Albert Thackrah, AIA. Our deep appreciation additionally goes to principals Dan Russoniello, AIA, LEED AP; and Chad Peterson, AIA for their continued support of and immeasurable contributions to the firm.

It takes a studio full of collaborative people, typically about 20 here at any given time, to consistently produce work at our desired and expected level of detail. Every one of our colleagues who either passed through this office or remained here for many years has contributed to 1,500 projects to date. With regard to this book effort, we want to thank especially architect and author Jim Garrison for his energetic discovery and articulation of the themes within our work; Henrika Dyck Taylor, the talented editor who clarified our collective ideas; Gina Dianna, our Marketing Director, for coordinating the people and the pieces involved in the production of the book; Tom Maciag and Rebecca Mah of Dyad Communications for the elegant book design and flawless execution; and finally Jeff Groff for writing so generously in his foreword about the firm's place in the world of design from his astute perspective as the Estate Historian at Winterthur.

Richard D. Buchanan and Peter C. Archer